SEE JESUS

To: Creighton
with love from Uncle Joel

Books by Kevin Johnson

Early Teen Devotionals

Can I Be a Christian Without Being Weird?
Could Someone Wake Me Up Before I Drool on the Desk?
Does Anybody Know What Planet My Parents Are From?
So Who Says I Have to Act My Age?
Was That a Balloon or Did Your Head Just Pop?
Who Should I Listen To?
Why Can't My Life Be a Summer Vacation?
Why Is God Looking for Friends?

Early Teen Discipleship

Get God: Make Friends With the King of the Universe
Wise Up: Stand Clear of the Unsmartness of Sin
Cross Train: Blast Through the Bible From Front to Back
Pray Hard: Talk to God With Total Confidence
See Jesus: Peer Into the Life and Mind of Your Master
Stick Tight: Glue Yourself to Godly Friends

Books for Youth

Catch the Wave!
Find Your Fit[1]
Find Your Fit Discovery Workbook[1]
Find Your Fit Leader's Guide[1]
God's Will, God's Best[2]
Jesus Among Other Gods: Youth Edition[3]
Look Who's Toast Now!
What Do Ya Know?
What's With the Dudes at the Door?[4]
What's With the Mutant in the Microscope?[4]

To find out more about Kevin Johnson's books or speaking availability, visit his Web site: www.thewave.org

[1]with Jane Kise [2]with Josh McDowell [3]with Ravi Zacharias [4]with James White

EARLY TEEN DISCIPLESHIP

Peer Into the Life and Mind of Your Master

SEE JESUS

Kevin Johnson

BETHANY HOUSE
MINNEAPOLIS, MINNESOTA

See Jesus
Copyright © 2001
Kevin Johnson

Cover by Lookout Design Group, Inc.

Published by Bethany House Publishers
A Ministry of Bethany Fellowship International
11400 Hampshire Avenue South
Bloomington, Minnesota 55438
www.bethanyhouse.com

Printed in the United States of America by
Bethany Press International, Bloomington, Minnesota 55438

Library of Congress Cataloging-in-Publication Data

Johnson, Kevin (Kevin Walter)
See Jesus : peer into the life and mind of your Master / by Kevin Johnson.
p. cm. — (Early teen discipleship)
Includes four sheets of Bible verses on removable, pocket-sized cards in back of book.
Summary: Presents the life of Jesus from a teenage perspective.
ISBN 0-7642-2433-6 (pbk.)
1. Jesus Christ—Biography—Juvenile literature. [1. Jesus Christ—Biography.] I. Title.
BT302 .J584 2001
232.9'01—dc21 2001002499

To Jim Maines

for showing us the bright shining glory of Jesus

KEVIN JOHNSON is the bestselling author or co-author of more than twenty books for youth, including *Can I Be a Christian Without Being Weird?* and *Catch the Wave!* A full-time author and speaker, he served as senior editor for adult nonfiction at Bethany House Publishers and pastored a group of more than four hundred sixth through ninth graders at Elmbrook Church in metro Milwaukee. While his training includes an M.Div. from Fuller Theological Seminary and a B.A. in English and Print Journalism from the University of Wisconsin–River Falls, his current interests include cycling, guitar, and shortwave radio. Kevin and his wife, Lyn, live in Minnesota with their three children—Nate, Karin, and Elise.

Contents

Part 3: Coaching the Clueless

Part 4: Growing His Followers

Part 5: Pointing Us Home

How to Use This Book

Welcome to *See Jesus*. This book is part of the EARLY TEEN DISCIPLESHIP series, better remembered by its clever initials, ETD. I wrote ETD as a follow-up to my series of bestselling devotionals—books like *Can I Be a Christian Without Being Weird?* and *Could Someone Wake Me Up Before I Drool on the Desk?* ETD has one aim: to help you take your next step in becoming wildly devoted to Jesus. If you're ready to work on a vital, heart-to-heart, sold-out relationship with God, this is your series.

The goal of *See Jesus* is to help you peer into the life and mind of your master. *See Jesus* prods you toward that goal through twenty-five Bible studies designed to make you think—okay, without *totally* breaking your brain. It will help you

- dig into Scripture on your own;
- feed on insights that you might not otherwise find;
- hit the heart issues that push you away from God or pull you closer to him.

You can pick your own pace—anything from a study a day to a study a week. But here's what you'll find in each study:

- Your first stop is BRAIN DRAIN—your spot at the beginning of each lesson to spout what you think.
- Then there's FLASHBACK—a bit of background so you better understand what's coming up.
- Don't skip over the BIBLE CHUNK—a hand-picked Bible passage to read.
- You get STUFF TO KNOW—questions to help you dig into what a passage means.
- There's INSIGHT—facts about the passage you might not figure out on your own.
- DA'SCOOP—definitions of weird words.
- And SIDELIGHT—other Bible verses that let you see the topic from a different angle.

The other big questions are, well . . .

- BIG QUESTIONS—your chance to apply what you have learned to your life.
- Each study wraps up with a DEEP THOT—a thought to chew on.

But that's not the end.

- There's STICKY STUFF—a Bible verse to jam into your brain juice.
- ACT ON IT—a way to do something with what you just learned.
- And DIG ON—another Bible passage to unearth if you want more.

And one more thing: There are cards in the back of the book for all the verses in STICKY STUFF, with a few bonus cards thrown in—since we'd already killed the tree.

If you've got a pencil and know how to use it, you're all set.

EXCEPT FOR ONE THING

You can study *See Jesus* on your own. But you can also work through this book with a friend or in a group. After every five studies there's a page called "Talk About It." Nope—you don't have to cover every question on the page. There are too many to answer, so pick the ones that matter most to you.

Whenever you do an ETD study with one friend or a bunch, keep in mind three goals—and three big questions to help you remember those goals. And nope—you don't have to actually ask those questions each time, because that would feel canned. But each time you meet you want to

- EMPATHIZE: *What's gone on since the last time you got together?* To "empathize" means to put yourself in someone else's shoes. Galatians 6:2 tells us to "carry each other's burdens" (NIV), or to "share each other's troubles and problems" (NLT). Whether you call them "highs and lows," "wows and pows," "uppers and downers," or "wins and wedgies," take time to celebrate and support each other by chatting through life's important happenings and offering simple, to-the-point prayers.
- ENCOURAGE: *Where are you at with Jesus?* Hebrews 3:13 says to "encourage one another daily. . . so that none of you may be hardened by sin's deceitfulness." Religious rules apart from a relationship with God are deadly. So instead be real: Are you

growing closer to or wandering away from the Lord you're learning to follow? Is anything tripping you up?

- EQUIP: *What one truth are you going to take away from today that will help you live closer to Jesus?* Second Timothy 3:16–17 promises that "All Scripture is inspired by God and is useful to teach us what is true and to make us realize what is wrong in our lives. It straightens us out and teaches us to do what is right. It is God's way of preparing us in every way, fully equipped for every good thing God wants us to do" (NLT). Don't leave your get-together without one point of truth that will make a difference in your life. It might not be the thought or verse that anyone else picks. But grab at least one truth—and hang on tight by letting it make a difference in your life.

Got it? Not only is *See Jesus* a study to do on your own, but better yet, it can help you grow your faith with your friends. You can pick a leader—a youth or adult—or take turns picking questions and talking through them as your time allows. Just keep the three big goals in mind.

Now you're ready. You can do it. Grow ahead and turn the page and get started.

PART 1

GROWING UP GOD

1. Silent Night, Holy Night

The arrival of Jesus

The wormhole *schwooops* shut behind you as you land with a thud—just in time to see Mary tuck baby Jesus into an animal's food trough. You eagerly look around to take in the rest of the first Christmas scene. But you don't hear any angels on high. And where are the shepherds watching their flocks by night or those three kings bearing gifts they traversed from afar? You've not stepped in any trace of those cattle lowing loud enough to wake poor baby Jesus. And when the little guy wails for his mommy, you know you've got really bad news for friends back home about that carol that claims "no crying he makes."

BRAIN DRAIN What would you expect to see if you could climb through time back to the scene of Jesus' birth?

FLASHBACK What you probably think of as *the* Christmas story is a mix of Luke 2 and Matthew 2 plus some thrown-in extras. See, the angels do speak to some shepherds—but that's an announcement made around the corner from where Jesus is born. The kings show up later, as you'll see in this Bible Chunk, but it's not clear that they're kings. Mary and Joseph did travel to Bethlehem and found no place to stay, but the stable where Christ was born isn't in the Bible. We do see a manger—a feeding trough—but Jesus could have been born in a cave or in a field under the stars. The stable—like the mooing of cows—is a guess. And there's a good chance the night wasn't silent. But for sure it was holy.

BIBLE CHUNK Read Matthew 2:1–12

(1) After Jesus was born in Bethlehem in Judea, during the time of King Herod, Magi from the east came to Jerusalem (2) and asked, "Where is the one who has been born king of the Jews? We saw his star in the east and have come to worship him."

(3) When King Herod heard this he was disturbed, and all Jerusalem with him. (4) When he had called together all the people's chief priests and teachers of the law, he asked them where the Christ was to be born. (5) "In Bethlehem in Judea," they replied, "for this is what the prophet has written:

(6) " 'But you, Bethlehem, in the land of Judah,
are by no means least among the rulers of Judah;
for out of you will come a ruler
who will be the shepherd of my people Israel.' "

(7) Then Herod called the Magi secretly and found out from them the exact time the star had appeared. (8) He sent them to Bethlehem and said, "Go and make a careful search for the child. As soon as you find him, report to me, so that I too may go and worship him."

(9) After they had heard the king, they went on their way, and the star they had seen in the east went ahead of them until it stopped over the place where the child was. (10) When they saw the star, they were overjoyed. (11) On coming to the house, they saw the child with his mother Mary, and they bowed down and worshiped him. Then they opened their treasures and presented him with gifts of gold and of incense and of myrrh. (12) And having been warned in a dream not to go back to Herod, they returned to their country by another route.

STUFF TO KNOW After Jesus is born, who comes searching for him? What are they looking to find (verses 1–2)?

INSIGHT Big problem. The country where Jesus is born—Israel—already has a king. Herod—a non-Jewish outsider who ruled from 37–4 B.C.—is so paranoid about threats to his throne that he murders his wife, three sons, mother-in-law, brother-in-law, and uncle. The quest for the "king of the Jews" disturbs Herod, and the whole city fears his rage.

Where is this king scheduled to be born (verses 5–6)?

SIDELIGHT Stunning factoid: Some seven centuries earlier, the birth of the "Christ" in Bethlehem was foretold (Micah 5:2).

What leads the "Magi" (say it "MAY-jai") to Jesus (verse 9)?

The Magi don't arrive empty-handed. What gifts do they bring (verse 11)?

INSIGHT Some Bible buffs see specific meanings in the gifts: gold because Jesus was king, incense because he was God, and myrrh because of his impending crucifixion. (Myrrh was an oil applied to Jesus after his death—see John 19:39–40).

INSIGHT If you want a true view of Jesus' birth, don't miss these for-sure details: (1) The Magi bring gifts fit for nobility, but the Bible doesn't clearly say that *they* are kings. Magi were best known for studying the stars. (2) The Magi didn't meet up with Jesus on the night of his birth. They visited a "child" in his "house." (3) There were three gifts, but the Bible doesn't say how many wise guys came to worship.

BIG QUESTIONS What do you think you would have thunk about the arrival of Jesus back then? Would you have spotted him as the King of the Universe come to rule earth?

Why do you suppose Jesus would show up as a baby?

SIDELIGHT The world's Savior might have been hard to spot as a tiny guy, but an angel made clear this baby's place in God's plans. In Matthew 1:21–23 he's called "Jesus" ("the Lord saves") and "Emmanuel" ("God with us").

DEEP THOT The eve of Jesus' birth might not have been exactly what you'd expect. With travelers bumping elbows looking for rooms and Mary moaning in labor, it wasn't likely a silent night. But it was a holy night. It fit God's purposes perfectly. It was all part of God's plan.

STICKY STUFF Memorize Matthew 2:11–12 as a reminder of how to bow before your King. There's a card in the back of *See Jesus* to help you out.

ACT ON IT Check your favorite Christmas carols against the facts of Jesus' arrival in Matthew 1–2 and Luke 1–2.

DIG ON You can catch the Bible's other major description of Jesus' birth in Luke 2:1–20.

2. Spiritual Freakazoid

When Jesus was your age

Blake's pastor is surprised when he whips out a Bible and clipboard. "Let me see if I've got this right," Blake says. "The incarnation of Jesus demonstrates once and for all that the imminence of God overshadows his transcendence, clearly leading us to conclude that God's choice to have a relationship with us overcomes our inability to understand the mysteries of his divinity?" Pastor Dumbstruck's mouth hangs open. "Hey, kid," he asks, "how old are you?"

BRAIN DRAIN Do you think it's weird for people your age to be interested in God? What's it look like to be *really* interested?

FLASHBACK Right after the last Bible Chunk, God warned Joseph in a dream that Herod would search out and destroy baby Jesus. Joseph, Mary, and Jesus fled to Egypt, and behind them Herod gave brutal orders to kill all the boys in Bethlehem under age two (Matthew 2:13–16). A little later, Jesus and his family moved homeward to a town called Nazareth (Matthew 2:23). And in this Bible Chunk, they're road-tripping to the biggest religious festival of the year. Jesus, his parents, and a mass of other people took off in a caravan to get there. But they weren't traveling via minivan. They had a full-day walk up to Jerusalem, Israel's political and spiritual capital. This Bible Chunk is your chance to see what Jesus was like at about your age. Spiritual freakazoid—or coolly close to God? You decide.

BIBLE CHUNK Read Luke 2:41–52

(41) Every year his parents went to Jerusalem for the Feast of the Passover. (42) When he was twelve years old, they went up to the Feast, according to the custom. (43) After the Feast was over, while his parents were returning home, the boy Jesus stayed behind in Jerusalem, but they were unaware of it. (44) Thinking he was in their company, they traveled on for a day. Then they began looking for him among their relatives and friends. (45) When they did not find him, they went back to Jerusalem to look for him. (46) After three days they found him in the temple courts, sitting among the teachers, listening to them and asking them questions. (47) Everyone who heard him was amazed at his understanding and his answers. (48) When his parents saw him, they were astonished. His mother said to him, "Son, why have you treated us like this? Your father and I have been anxiously searching for you."

(49) "Why were you searching for me?" he asked. "Didn't you know I had to be in my Father's house?" (50) But they did not understand what he was saying to them.

(51) Then he went down to Nazareth with them and was obedient to them. But his mother treasured all these things in her heart. (52) And Jesus grew in wisdom and stature, and in favor with God and men.

STUFF TO KNOW So how old is Jesus in this snapshot (verse 42)? And what does he pull on his parents (verse 43)?

INSIGHT Given how groups traveled back in Bible times, it's not hard to picture how Jesus likely got left behind. He's at an in-between age where his dad thinks he's traveling with the women and children, and his mom figures he's with the men and older boys. Oops.

It takes a day to notice Jesus is missing, a day to get back to Jerusalem, and a day to find him among the crowds. So what's Jesus been up to for three days (verse 46)?

Does it sound like Jesus was throwing spit wads during the Sunday school lesson? How is he acting (verse 47)?

INSIGHT The folks who hung out at the temple wouldn't be wowed by the questions of a little boy. They were accustomed to the probing logic of ancient academies, and Jesus apparently displayed brilliant spiritual insight. And he does more than ask questions. He gives answers and spots things in Scripture the religious hotshots had never heard of.

Hmmm . . . but back to those worried parents. How does his mom react (verse 48)?

And how does Jesus answer her (verse 49)?

INSIGHT Jesus is clearly aware that he's God's Son, and he hints that his parents—since they knew that too—should have realized where he was. And here's what it looks like to be twelve and live all-out for God: Jesus has huge insight into God, but those spiritual smarts display themselves as he obeys his parents.

So how does Luke 2:52 sum up Jesus' growth?

BIG QUESTIONS What's the lesson of this Bible Chunk—that it's okay to ditch your parents as long as you're having deep discussions at church?

You might never have stumped the older Christians around you. But how badly do you want to get to know God?

DEEP THOT You don't have to have a mouthful of religious mumbo jumbo to show that you're way-interested in God. Jesus asked hard questions. He thought hard about answers. That's a *want-to-grow* attitude. Jesus isn't some spiritual freakazoid. He's spiritually cool.

STICKY STUFF Stick Luke 2:52 in your brain and aim for the same sort of growth you spot in Jesus.

ACT ON IT Ask your parents how long you'd be grounded if you did what Jesus did.

DIG ON This is the Bible's only record of Jesus at about your age. But see how Hebrews 5:8 describes everything Jesus was learning.

3. The Human Drum Roll

John the Baptist prepares the way for Jesus

We know that a choir of dazzling angels announced Jesus' birth—and that after a little bit, wise men knelt before him and brought gifts fit for a king. But other than showing Jesus baffling his elders at the temple, the Bible says nothing about Jesus' growing up. Like most guys at his time, he took up his father's trade—carpentry (Mark 6:3). And when it came time for Jesus to openly begin his ministry on earth, God brought in a one-man advertising agency. A human drum roll. A desert-dwelling holy man. A straight-shooting guy known for absolute purity. But this John guy had his quirks.

BRAIN DRAIN If you were God, how would you have launched Jesus' work on planet Earth?

FLASHBACK The Old Testament—the front half of the Bible—said lots about who Jesus would be and what he would do (more on that in study 6 of *See Jesus*). But the Old Testament also predicted the arrival of a guy named John. He was the one Isaiah said would cry out in the desert, "Prepare the way for the Lord!" (Isaiah 40:3). This isn't the John who wrote the Bible book named, um, *John*, but actually a cousin of Jesus best known as a desert-dwelling holy man who wore camel-hair clothes and lived on wild honey and big-bug locusts. And he had one message: Get ready for God to get in your face.

BIBLE CHUNK Read Matthew 3:13–17

> (13) Then Jesus came from Galilee to the Jordan to be baptized by John. (14) But John tried to deter him, saying, "I need to be baptized by you, and do you come to me?"

(15) Jesus replied, "Let it be so now; it is proper for us to do this to fulfill all righteousness." Then John consented.

(16) As soon as Jesus was baptized, he went up out of the water. At that moment heaven was opened, and he saw the Spirit of God descending like a dove and lighting on him. (17) And a voice from heaven said, "This is my Son, whom I love; with him I am well pleased."

STUFF TO KNOW Why did Jesus walk a long way to see John (verse 13)? What's that all about?

DA'SCOOP The back half of the Bible—the New Testament—was first written in Greek. The word behind "baptism" was an everyday word that meant "to wash." But baptism came to mean way more than that. John dunks people in the Jordan River to show they're "repenting," consciously turning from the wrong things they've done.

When Jesus wants to be baptized, is John just being rude? Does he see his cousin as a spiritual big shot (verse 14)?

INSIGHT Double nope! John's reluctance comes from humility. He insists *he* needs to be baptized by *Jesus*. A little earlier John wouldn't dunk some religious leaders because he doubted they were sincere about ditching evil (Matthew 3:7–10). John has known Jesus since birth, and he knows Jesus has no need for a ritual that symbolizes scrubbing clean of sin.

Jesus insists right back. What reason does he supply for John to baptize him (verse 15)?

INSIGHT "John," Jesus more or less says, "it's the right thing to do." Jesus has no sins he needs to wash away. But as the Savior who will soon die for the human race, he's acting as a servant and saying, "Look, I'm one of you."

Something huge happens right after Jesus comes up out of the water. What (verse 16)?

INSIGHT Big news: This is a Bible Chunk where you plainly spot the Father, Son, and Holy Spirit in one scene. They're different, yet so closely connected that they're somehow the same. Each is fully God. But they're not three separate Gods. They're *one being* (God), in *three persons* (Father, Son, and Holy Spirit). They're a "tri-unity," what the Bible buffs dub the "Trinity." Tough to grasp, but a key to all of Scripture.

Booming from heaven, God speaks aloud, something he only does in two other New Testament spots—Luke 9:35 and John 12:28. What's so important for him to say (verse 17)?

INSIGHT Got your ears on to those three things? God says Jesus is his Son. That he loves Jesus. And that he's pleased with Jesus.

SIDELIGHT Not much later, John says one more crucial thing about Jesus. He calls him "the Lamb of God, who takes away the sin of the world!" (John 1:29). In the Old Testament, lambs and other animals were killed to pay the penalty for people's sins. He drops a not-so-subtle hint: Jesus was going to act as the ultimate Lamb and pay the price for the world's sins.

BIG QUESTIONS John is out in the desert, dining on jumbotronic grasshoppers—and he's announcing that Jesus is the Savior arriving on planet Earth. Would you have believed him? Why? Or why not?

These events happen as the big spiritual mission of Jesus' life starts to heat up. What do you suppose it did for Jesus to have his Father's satisfaction shouted from heaven?

DEEP THOT Wrap together everything you hear about Jesus because of John the Baptist, and you get a couple huge hints about who Jesus is: He's God's beloved son, set to sacrifice himself for the world's sins.

STICKY STUFF Stuff Matthew 3:17 in your head to remember why Jesus is the one to follow.

ACT ON IT John the Baptist caused people to think hard about what they'd done to offend God and hurt people. Tell God about bad attitudes and actions you'd like to ditch—and remember the promise of 1 John 1:9: "If we confess our sins to [God], he is faithful and just to forgive us and to cleanse us from every wrong" (NLT).

DIG ON Read more about John the Baptist's one-of-a-kind ways in Luke 3.

4. Cosmic Football

The temptation of Jesus

You say "Jesus" and the first thing that barges into some people's brains are words like "weak," "wimp," and "wuss." They figure this good guy must be a mama's boy who would lose an arm-wrestling match to the six-year-old kid next door. But Jesus is anything but a pasty-faced priss.

BRAIN DRAIN What would you say to someone who claims Jesus is a wimp—or that faith is for weaklings?

FLASHBACK Hmm . . . maybe you think that Jesus the boy (a.k.a. "Twelve-year-old Spiritual Whiz Kid) was a goody-goody who never had a chance to mess up. Or that John the Baptist saw only total goodness in Jesus because Jesus the teenager really faced the possibility of being evil. But Jesus *never* had it easy. Hebrews 4:15 says he was "tempted in every way, just as we are—yet was without sin." This next Bible Chunk shows that his battles were nastier than anything *we* ever face—and that Jesus is tougher than we imagine.

BIBLE CHUNK Read Matthew 4:1–11

(1) Then Jesus was led by the Spirit into the desert to be tempted by the devil. (2) After fasting forty days and forty nights, he was hungry. (3) The tempter came to him and said, "If you are the Son of God, tell these stones to become bread."

(4) Jesus answered, "It is written: 'Man does not live on bread alone, but on every word that comes from the mouth of God.' "

(5) Then the devil took him to the holy city and had him stand on the
highest point of the temple. (6) "If you are the Son of God," he said,
"throw yourself down. For it is written:

" 'He will command his angels concerning you,
and they will lift you up in their hands,
so that you will not strike your foot against a stone.' "

(7) Jesus answered him, "It is also written: 'Do not put the Lord your
God to the test.' "

(8) Again, the devil took him to a very high mountain and showed him
all the kingdoms of the world and their splendor. (9) "All this I will give
you," he said, "if you will bow down and worship me."

(10) Jesus said to him, "Away from me, Satan! For it is written: 'Worship
the Lord your God, and serve him only.' "

(11) Then the devil left him, and angels came and attended him.

STUFF TO KNOW Who's going to tempt Jesus (verse 1)?

SIDELIGHT The Bible is clear that temptation doesn't always come straight from Satan. Often it's the dark underside of our hearts that gets us hankering for the wrong things (James 1:14–15). The Holy Spirit leads Jesus to a place where Jesus will fellowship with his Father—but also face gargantuan temptations. Yet God himself never tempts anyone (James 1:13). Jesus is getting the chance to prove he's as obedient under intense pressure as he is in normal life.

What's Jesus been doing—or not doing—for forty days (verse 2)? What's that first temptation all about (verse 3)?

INSIGHT After Jesus had spent more than a month minus food to devote himself to prayer, Satan suggests he miraculously bake himself some bread. Turning a rock into food would be using his earth-shattering powers to meet his good needs in a bad way—as in *outside God's plan*.

Surprised that Jesus doesn't just point an all-powerful finger at Satan and smoke him? So how does Jesus fight back? What book does Jesus quote from (verse 4)?

What is doing a swan dive off the temple's peak supposed to prove (verses 5–7)?

INSIGHT *Not* making a big splat would make a big splash. The temptation? To woo the crowds by a powerful yet pointless miracle.

Satan takes Jesus to another high-up spot. What does he promise Jesus this time? On what condition (verse 9)?

And with that, Jesus sends Satan off with one last kick to the head. What does he say (verse 10)?

BIG QUESTIONS Have you ever pondered the fact that Christ was genuinely tempted to do wrong just like you? What's surprising about that?

INSIGHT You might wonder how someone who lived in way-back society could be "tempted in every way, just as we are." Get this: The ancient world was way more rude and crude than your world. On top of that, Jesus was like the football in a cosmic contest between good and evil. He got tossed, squeezed, and booted from birth to death. But he stayed pumped up.

From what you see in this Bible Chunk, what's the best way to fight back when you feel big-time tempted?

DEEP THOT Here's a thought: When you feel tempted, you have access to the same weapon Jesus used: God's Word. God has outfitted you with the planet's most powerful temptation blaster: the true facts of life found in the Bible.

STICKY STUFF Hang on tight to Matthew 4:4 to know where real fun comes from.

ACT ON IT Think of an area where you face frequent temptation. Ask a more mature Christian to help you find verses that help you battle back.

DIG ON Knowing that Jesus knows exactly what you're going through when you're tempted gives you one more reason to stay obedient to God. Check out how Jesus helps in Hebrews 4:14–16.

5. In the Very Beginning

Jesus' true identity

When you want to see Jesus, the place to go is the first four books of the New Testament. Each of these Gospels—Matthew, Mark, Luke, and John—describes Jesus from a slightly different angle. Matthew wants to show his fellow Jews that Jesus is the Messiah promised in the Old Testament. Mark offers straightforward accounts for people lacking that background. Luke writes to non-Jews like himself, highlighting how Jesus gets along with outsiders and outcasts. But none of these books starts at the *very* beginning, even though that's a very fine place to start. John starts by showing Jesus even before he came to earth. And he tells you right up front who Jesus is.

BRAIN DRAIN So what would you tell someone who asked you to describe Jesus?

FLASHBACK First thing you spot in this Bible Chunk: It calls Jesus "the Word." The Greeks saw "the Word" as the brains behind the universe. The Jews—God's Old Testament people—used "the Word" to refer to God. John managed to find a term to explain Jesus that meant something immensely huge to both big groups of readers.

BIBLE CHUNK Read John 1:1–14

(1) In the beginning was the Word, and the Word was with God, and the Word was God. (2) He was with God in the beginning.

(3) Through him all things were made; without him nothing was made that has been made. (4) In him was life, and that life was the light of men. (5) The light shines in the darkness, but the darkness has not understood it.

(6) There came a man who was sent from God; his name was John. (7) He came as a witness to testify concerning that light, so that through him all men might believe. (8) He himself was not the light; he came only as a witness to the light. (9) The true light that gives light to every man was coming into the world.

(10) He was in the world, and though the world was made through him, the world did not recognize him. (11) He came to that which was his own, but his own did not receive him. (12) Yet to all who received him, to those who believed in his name, he gave the right to become children of God—(13) children born not of natural descent, nor of human decision or a husband's will, but born of God.

(14) The Word became flesh and made his dwelling among us. We have seen his glory, the glory of the One and Only, who came from the Father, full of grace and truth.

STUFF TO KNOW So what's that name John gives to Jesus? And what does John say about Jesus (verse 1)?

INSIGHT That "beginning" thing doesn't refer to a particular moment in time but a timeless eternity. So first, Jesus *didn't have a beginning*. He always existed. Second, to be "with God" means to be God's face-to-face equal. And third, Jesus is no cheapo minigod or hyped-up human. He's totally God.

What good four-letter thing do you find when you are "in him" (verse 4)? Tougher one: What good will that do you (verses 4–5)?

INSIGHT When the Bible talks about you being "in" Jesus, it means you're in a real relationship with him. Jesus says that because he's the "light of the world" then "whoever follows me will never walk in darkness, but will have the light of life" (John 8:12). As long as you stick close to him, you'll see—you'll have true knowledge of God and of life.

Skip down this Bible Chunk a bit. What does it say the Word did (verse 14)?

- The Word became . . .

- The Word made his dwelling . . .

And what did we see in Jesus (verse 14)?

SIDELIGHT Staggering! It's God in a bod. Jesus is "the image of the invisible God" (Colossians 1:15 NLT) and "the fullness of God . . . in a human body" (2:9 NLT). Jesus makes his own astoundingly clear claims to be God in places like John 8:58–59 and Revelation 22:12–13.

You'd think that everyone who saw Jesus would immediately believe in him. But how did some folks react to Jesus (verses 10–11)?

How do others respond? And what does God do for them (verse 12)?

INSIGHT To receive Jesus is to believe *who he is* and *what he's done for you.*

BIG QUESTIONS So is it hard to believe God came to earth as a human being—and that through Jesus you see who God is? Why or why not?

DEEP THOT John says that the whole reason he wrote his account of Jesus is for you to come to believe in Jesus and find life in him (John 20:31). You might have believed in Jesus for a long time, trusting that he is God, that he cares for you, and that he died in your place. But you can also start a relationship with him right now. You can say to God, "I believe that Jesus is the Savior you sent to die for my sins. I want to follow you—to live with you as my Lord." That's a simple start. But it's how you know you're friends with God. And it's how you start to see Jesus in ways deeper than you can imagine.

STICKY STUFF John 1:12 is a perfect passage to rattle around in your head. It's all about receiving Jesus.

ACT ON IT If you've never made a concrete decision that you want the forgiveness and friendship God offers in Jesus, do it now. And tell someone you did!

DIG ON You've read the first words of John's book. Now read the last: John 20:24–31.

Talk About It • 1

EMPATHIZE: What's going on in your life?
ENCOURAGE: How are you doing with Jesus?
EQUIP: What one truth will you take home today?

- What would you expect to see if you could climb through time back to the scene of Jesus' birth? (Study 1)
- Why do you suppose Jesus would show up as a baby? (Study 1)
- Do you think it's weird for people your age to be really interested in God? (Study 2)
- How badly do you want to get to know God? (Study 2)
- Would you have believed John the Baptist telling you that Jesus was going to save planet Earth? (Study 3)
- What does it mean that Jesus is going to be "the Lamb of God"? (Study 3)
- What would you say to someone who claims Jesus is a wimp—or that faith is for weaklings? (Study 4)
- From what you see in Jesus' temptation by Satan, what's the best way to fight back when you feel big-time tempted? (Study 4)
- What's so unusual about Jesus? Who is he? (Study 5)
- What's it mean to "receive Jesus"? (Study 5)

PART 2

MAKING A SCENE

6. Tourist Trap

Jesus cleans out the temple

"I can't stand going to church," Mikala fumes. "It's because of my old Sunday school teacher. Everyone slaps him on the back and says how much they love him, but I can't stand how he treats his wife and kids. Almost every week I see him screaming in the car as they pull into church. I can't be the only one who notices. The other adults at church are just as bad for not doing something about it."

BRAIN DRAIN So how do you react when you see someone acting like a hypocrite?

FLASHBACK Jesus once said that dealing with hypocrites is like yanking weeds from a field. Act carelessly, and you'll destroy good people along with the bad (Matthew 13:2–30). But in this Bible Chunk you see Jesus chase off hypocrites who had made the temple into a crooked bank—and a stinking animal market. Jesus is heading to Jerusalem for that same Passover festival where his parents lost him almost two decades before. The problems at the temple were nothing new. But Jesus cleaned up in a way no one had ever done before.

BIBLE CHUNK Read John 2:13–25

(13) When it was almost time for the Jewish Passover, Jesus went up to Jerusalem. (14) In the temple courts he found men selling cattle, sheep and doves, and others sitting at tables exchanging money. (15) So he made

a whip out of cords, and drove all from the temple area, both sheep and cattle; he scattered the coins of the money changers and overturned their tables. (16) To those who sold doves he said, "Get these out of here! How dare you turn my Father's house into a market!"

(17) His disciples remembered that it is written: "Zeal for your house will consume me."

(18) Then the Jews demanded of him, "What miraculous sign can you show us to prove your authority to do all this?"

(19) Jesus answered them, "Destroy this temple, and I will raise it again in three days."

(20) The Jews replied, "It has taken forty-six years to build this temple, and you are going to raise it in three days?" (21) But the temple he had spoken of was his body. (22) After he was raised from the dead, his disciples recalled what he had said. Then they believed the Scripture and the words that Jesus had spoken.

(23) Now while he was in Jerusalem at the Passover Feast, many people saw the miraculous signs he was doing and believed in his name. (24) But Jesus would not entrust himself to them, for he knew all men. (25) He did not need man's testimony about man, for he knew what was in a man.

STUFF TO KNOW Family-of-Jesus tidbit: Just before this Bible Chunk you spot not only Jesus' mother but his brothers (John 2:12). Later John says his brothers "thought he was out of his mind" and "did not believe in him" (John 7:5), although after Jesus' resurrection his brother James became the key leader of the church in Jerusalem (Acts 15:13–21). Since Joseph isn't seen in this scene, many Bible buffs assume he's died.

What does Jesus find in the temple (verse 14)?

INSIGHT The merchants think nothing of their trade. They sell animals required for sacrifices at the temple, providing a we-bring-it-you-buy-it-and-burn-it convenience for worshipers who don't want to drag their animals to the temple from afar. Other merchants exchange foreign currencies for money acceptable to temple authorities—although for a crookedly expensive fee. Yet the all-important *place* where they were selling was what really angered Jesus. Their activities take place in a sacred worship space.

So what does Jesus do (verse 15)? What does he say (verse 16)?

The business guys rage at Jesus for disrupting their bustling, hustling business. What do they want from Jesus (verse 18)?

INSIGHT When everyone wants to know what gives Jesus the right to tip tables, they demand the kind of miracle he's doing in verse 23. Jesus says he's out to do a bigger miracle—and to disrupt the temple in an even bigger way. The temple was the centerpiece of Jewish religion, but here Jesus is saying, "Now *I* am the center of what it means to worship God." They figure Jesus means the lavish stone temple, which had been under construction longer than most of them had been alive. Even his disciples don't understand what Jesus says. That "forty-six years," by the way, dates this event around A.D. 26.

BIG QUESTIONS But what do you think about what Jesus did?

Or here's the flip side: What do you think of religion that looks the other way when hypocrisy runs wild?

SIDELIGHT Jesus had harsh words for people who made a mockery of spiritual stuff—especially those who put on a pretty front on the outside even though they were filthy messes on the inside. As Jesus' ministry spread, his harshest words were for religious leaders hostile to his message. He aimed frequent criticism at the "Pharisees," the most religious people of Jesus' day and a group known for their ultracareful rule-keeping—and their scorn for all the other "sinners" in society. Read in Matthew 23 how Jesus hit hard at their hypocrisy.

DEEP THOT Warning: We don't have the authority that Jesus had as God in the flesh to exercise that kind of judgment on religious hypocrites. (In other words, don't try table-tossing at your church.) But you can put a fast halt to hypocrisy when you see it in your own life.

STICKY STUFF Get heated along with Jesus: Memorize John 2:17.

ACT ON IT Tell God you want to be pure to the core—and ask him to change you from the inside out (Matthew 23:25–26).

DIG ON See Matthew 23:1–36 for some of the hot words Jesus aimed at hypocrites.

7. Insert Head and Slam

God wants to know you

Jacob stared at the ground. "I just don't get it," he confessed to his youth pastor. "Everyone else always understands what you're talking about. When we get talking about spiritual stuff I feel like I have to slam my head in a door and hope something leaks out. Maybe if you explained it all one more time . . ."

BRAIN DRAIN If you could sneak up to Jesus and ask him a question without anyone hearing, what would you ask?

FLASHBACK You probably know this Bible Chunk—or at least part of it. It wraps around what's likely the best-known verse in the Bible, John 3:16: "For God so loved the world that he gave his one and only Son, that whoever believes in him shall not perish but have eternal life." Jesus spoke those words to a member of the Pharisees—that ultrareligious group that usually opposed him. But this guy is different. He's looking for God.

BIBLE CHUNK Read John 3:1–18

(1) Now there was a man of the Pharisees named Nicodemus, a member of the Jewish ruling council. (2) He came to Jesus at night and said, "Rabbi, we know you are a teacher who has come from God. For no one could perform the miraculous signs you are doing if God were not with him."

(3) In reply Jesus declared, "I tell you the truth, no one can see the kingdom of God unless he is born again."

(4) "How can a man be born when he is old?" Nicodemus asked.

"Surely he cannot enter a second time into his mother's womb to be born!"

(5) Jesus answered, "I tell you the truth, no one can enter the kingdom of God unless he is born of water and the Spirit. (6) Flesh gives birth to flesh, but the Spirit gives birth to spirit. (7) You should not be surprised at my saying, 'You must be born again.' (8) The wind blows wherever it pleases. You hear its sound, but you cannot tell where it comes from or where it is going. So it is with everyone born of the Spirit."

(9) "How can this be?" Nicodemus asked.

(10) "You are Israel's teacher," said Jesus, "and do you not understand these things? (11) I tell you the truth, we speak of what we know, and we testify to what we have seen, but still you people do not accept our testimony. (12) I have spoken to you of earthly things and you do not believe; how then will you believe if I speak of heavenly things? (13) No one has ever gone into heaven except the one who came from heaven—the Son of Man. (14) Just as Moses lifted up the snake in the desert, so the Son of Man must be lifted up, (15) that everyone who believes in him may have eternal life.

(16) "For God so loved the world that he gave his one and only Son, that whoever believes in him shall not perish but have eternal life. (17) For God did not send his Son into the world to condemn the world, but to save the world through him. (18) Whoever believes in him is not condemned, but whoever does not believe stands condemned already because he has not believed in the name of God's one and only Son."

STUFF TO KNOW

Why would Nicodemus show up at night (verses 1–2)?

What does Nic believe about Jesus (verse 2)?

So how does Jesus respond to Nicodemus's nice words (verse 3)?

DA'SCOOP Jesus' reply takes a jump from what Nicodemus said to where Jesus knows he needs to go. And that all-important phrase "born again" can also be read as "born from above." Nicodemus misses that spiritual meaning, because he's wondering how a baby can squeeze back into its mother's womb.

What does Jesus say it takes to "enter the kingdom of God" (verses 5–8)? Any guesses on what all that means?

INSIGHT Being born "of the Spirit" means that to get to know God the Holy Spirit has to rework your heart and mind. The "water" part is another way to say the clean-up job the Spirit does in people—see Titus 3:5 for more. And the Spirit is like the wind: You can't see it, but you spot its effects.

When Jesus says, "You don't understand this stuff?" he's referring not just to Nicodemus but to all of Israel's teachers. So why did God send Jesus (verse 16)?

SIDELIGHT That "snake in the desert" line refers to a famous Old Testament event. Check out Numbers 21:8–9 to see the similarities to Jesus being "lifted up" on the cross.

What cool stuff does Jesus promise to people who believe in him (verses 16, 18)?

BIG QUESTIONS So would Jesus' statements have left you baffled? How does John 3:16 kind of sum up the big point of what Jesus said to Nicodemus?

Is getting to know God something you do because you *want* to—or because you *have* to?

DEEP THOT The merchants in the temple saw religion as a path to riches. The Pharisees saw religion as a Ping-Pong game batting around rules and big religious thoughts. Jesus wanted Nicodemus to know that religion is way more than that. Jesus came to planet Earth to tell you that God wants to have a relationship with you—and with the rest of the world he made.

STICKY STUFF If you know John 3:16, you know the big point of the Bible.

ACT ON IT Make a list of all the rules you have to follow in a day. Which are hard? Which are easy? Why?

DIG ON Grab a gander at Titus 2:11–14 and 3:1–8 for another explanation of how God works inside you.

8. Big Promise

Jesus fulfills prophecy

You wouldn't buy this promise if you heard it mouthed by a politician. But look what the Ultimate Ruler of the Universe said about the Savior he would send—a pledge made in the Old Testament several hundred years before the Savior was to show up: "For to us a child is born, to us a son is given, and the government will be on his shoulders. And he will be called Wonderful Counselor, Mighty God, Everlasting Father, Prince of Peace. Of the increase of his government and peace there will be no end. He will reign on David's throne and over his kingdom, establishing and upholding it with justice and righteousness from that time on and forever. The zeal of the Lord Almighty will accomplish this" (Isaiah 9:6–7).

BRAIN DRAIN How do you know when to believe a big promise?

FLASHBACK You saw Jesus at his baptism. Right after his baptism he hoofed into the wilderness and was tempted by the arch evildoer. And in this next Bible Chunk Jesus teaches at his hometown synagogue—the local Jewish assembly.

BIBLE CHUNK Read Luke 4:14–21

(14) Jesus returned to Galilee in the power of the Spirit, and news about him spread through the whole countryside. (15) He taught in their synagogues, and everyone praised him.

(16) He went to Nazareth, where he had been brought up, and on the

Sabbath day he went into the synagogue, as was his custom. And he stood up to read. (17) The scroll of the prophet Isaiah was handed to him. Unrolling it, he found the place where it is written:

(18) "The Spirit of the Lord is on me,
because he has anointed me
to preach good news to the poor.
He has sent me to proclaim freedom for the prisoners
and recovery of sight for the blind,
to release the oppressed,
(19) to proclaim the year of the Lord's favor."

(20) Then he rolled up the scroll, gave it back to the attendant and sat down. The eyes of everyone in the synagogue were fastened on him, (21) and he began by saying to them, "Today this scripture is fulfilled in your hearing."

STUFF TO KNOW Jesus had been out and about in the countryside of his home region. What's he been doing? What did people think of him (verse 15)?

When he got to his hometown, where did he go? Why? And what did he stand up to do (verse 16)?

INSIGHT The Bible doesn't say whether the chunk Jesus read—Isaiah 61:1–2—was scheduled to be read that day or hand-picked by Jesus. Either way he had something huge to say.

That chunk Jesus read is another huge Old Testament promise—what Bible buffs call a "prophecy"—that God would send a Savior. So what's this Savior going to do (verses 18–19)?

When Jesus sat down, it didn't mean he was set to shut up. It meant he was going to teach. What does he say to all his townsfolk (verse 21)?

SIDELIGHT The hugeness of Jesus' words might zing over your head. But all of his hearers know he's just read a statement about the Savior that God promised to send—and that Jesus has claimed to be the fulfillment of the promise. Anyone could make that claim. But it's truly astounding that this is one of dozens of Old Testament predictions that came true in the New Testament in Jesus—factoids foretold with incredible detail hundreds of years before his arrival, most of them completely beyond his control. Here are just a few of these Bible prophecies:

PREDICTED:	FULFILLED IN JESUS:
be a descendant of King David 2 Samuel 7:12	Matthew 1:17
be born in the town of Bethlehem Micah 5:2–5	Luke 2:4–7
be born to a virgin Isaiah 7:14	Matthew 1:21
be silent before his accusers Isaiah 53:7	Matthew 27:12–19
be pierced in his side Zechariah 12:10	John 19:34
rise from the dead Psalm 16:10	Mark 16:6

Bible prophecies say lots more about God's servant. But here's one especially crucial thing: Isaiah 53:5 foretold, "He was pierced for our transgressions, he was crushed for our iniquities; the punishment that brought us peace was upon him, and by his wounds we are healed." God would send a Savior—but a Savior who would die the death humankind deserves.

BIG QUESTIONS Why would God tell all this stuff about Jesus beforehand?

Looking at those promises God has made, what do you think of the Savior he promised to send?

DEEP THOT All those prophecies Jesus flawlessly fulfilled were meant to help people recognize the Savior—the "Christ" or the "anointed" or "chosen" one—that God would send. They're also a huge proof that Jesus was who he claimed to be. God didn't just spew big promises like someone running for election. In Jesus, he did what he said he would do.

STICKY STUFF Stick Luke 4:18–19 in your brain if you want to remember what kind of Savior God was gonna send.

ACT ON IT Ask in your church library or Christian bookstore for a book with a complete list of prophecies fulfilled in Jesus.

DIG ON Dive into any of those prophecies listed in this study that came true in Jesus.

9. That's Downright Unneighborly

Jesus preaches in his hometown

Your front door swings open and on the step stands your eight-year-old neighbor in a snappy little power suit. "Hi!" she gushes. "I'm working on my Bible prophecy badges. See, I'm trying to fulfill all the Old Testament predictions about the Savior that God is sending to rescue the world. For every prophecy I fulfill I earn a badge—and if I get enough, people will think I'm God! I wasn't born in Bethlehem, but I've done *very* well since then." You're speechless. Well, not quite. "Emily," you ask, "aren't you supposed to be selling cookies?"

BRAIN DRAIN Forget for a minute that you know all about Jesus. How would you react if a kid down the block thought he or she was God?

FLASHBACK Here's the tail end of the last Bible Chunk you read—plus the rest of the story. Jesus had declared he was fulfilling one of God's major Old Testament promises. But you won't believe the hot welcome Jesus got in Nazareth, his hometown.

BIBLE CHUNK Read Luke 4:20–32

(20) Then he rolled up the scroll, gave it back to the attendant and sat down. The eyes of everyone in the synagogue were fastened on him,

(21) and he began by saying to them, "Today this scripture is fulfilled in your hearing."

(22) All spoke well of him and were amazed at the gracious words that came from his lips. "Isn't this Joseph's son?" they asked.

(23) Jesus said to them, "Surely you will quote this proverb to me: 'Physician, heal yourself! Do here in your hometown what we have heard that you did in Capernaum.' "

(24) "I tell you the truth," he continued, "no prophet is accepted in his hometown. (25) I assure you that there were many widows in Israel in Elijah's time, when the sky was shut for three and a half years and there was a severe famine throughout the land. (26) Yet Elijah was not sent to any of them, but to a widow in Zarephath in the region of Sidon. (27) And there were many in Israel with leprosy in the time of Elisha the prophet, yet not one of them was cleansed—only Naaman the Syrian."

(28) All the people in the synagogue were furious when they heard this. (29) They got up, drove him out of the town, and took him to the brow of the hill on which the town was built, in order to throw him down the cliff. (30) But he walked right through the crowd and went on his way.

(31) Then he went down to Capernaum, a town in Galilee, and on the Sabbath began to teach the people. (32) They were amazed at his teaching, because his message had authority.

STUFF TO KNOW At the beginning of this Bible Chunk it sounds like Jesus is a smash hit. At least he's got their intense attention. So what are they amazed by (verse 22)?

Instead of defending his claims, Jesus hears these comments and hoofs straight to what they're thinking. What does he know they want him to do (verse 23)?

SIDELIGHT People don't just know Jesus' earthly father, Joseph. They know his brothers and sisters (Mark 6:1–6) and everything else nosy neighbors would know. At the start of this chunk they smile with amazement. Yet they find it hard to believe there's anything special about Jesus—much less that he's the Savior sent from God. They want him to do the jaw-dropping things they'd heard he'd done in Capernaum. (Mark 1–2 tells about some of Jesus' early miracles there.)

INSIGHT Instead of giving the crowd time to respond, Jesus explains how the Old Testament prophet Elijah went and provided food not for a Jewish widow but one from Sidon, and how he healed a non-Jew named Naaman. He's saying, in other words, that in the past God led one of his big-time servants to do miracles outside his homeland and—don't miss this—among people hated by Jesus' old neighbors in Nazareth.

So just how mad is the crowd? What do they do (verse 29)?

How does Jesus solve this uptight situation (verse 30)?

SIDELIGHT Big point: Just before the cross—when Jesus is arrested, in fact—he tells his capturers that he could call down "twelve legions of angels" (in case you're counting, that's 72,000) to rescue him (Matthew 26:53). This isn't his time. He's not going to die now just because a mob wants to do him in.

BIG QUESTIONS When have people slammed you—and said you couldn't do something—just because they thought they knew you?

Put yourself in Jesus' sandals. How hard do you think it was for him to preach to the people in his hometown?

Why do you think those townsfolk rejected Jesus? What's at the root of their bad attitude?

When you try to live all-out for God, people might mock your spiritual intensity. How is the nastiness you might face like the hostility Jesus faced?

DEEP THOT Not only are Jesus' neighbors wondering how the boy down the block turned into such a big shot, but they don't like him telling them that God loves people they don't. Jesus has a simple solution: He moves on to areas that want his help (Luke 4:31–32).

STICKY STUFF Tuck the wise words of Luke 4:24 in your head. They'll explain a lot of wacko situations in life.

ACT ON IT Apologize to someone you've jumped to conclusions about.

DIG ON Read John 10:17–18 for Jesus' explanation of why he won't expire before his time.

10. If You Were in Movies

Jesus gathers his disciples

A violin solo swells above the sound of monks droning an eerie yet inspiring *ah ah ah*. The camera catches Jesus in the distance, striding toward a softball game, robe billowing in the breeze. *Scene change:* The view zooms to you, standing at bat. *Scene change:* Jesus nears home plate. *Scene change:* You see Jesus standing in front of you. The monk music soars. *Scene change:* The eyes of Jesus pierce you . . . he raises an eyebrow . . . he says "follow me" with a voice deep enough to blow a subwoofer. The camera pans wide . . . and you . . . you drop your bat and follow a stranger you've never met.

BRAIN DRAIN How would you react if Jesus got right in your face and said, "Drop everything and follow me"?

FLASHBACK Maybe you picture Jesus' disciples lured into following him by some sci-fi-spaceship-tractor-beam stare, pulled to serve a guy they knew nothing about. Maybe that's how it looks in movies—or how it sounds in sermons—but the Bible gives some big signs that his followers knew who was asking them to drop everything and follow. The fishermen who follow Jesus in Matthew 4:18–27, for example, met him back in John 1:35–51. And in this Bible Chunk—when a tax collector named Levi follows—Jesus has already been teaching and doing miracles in the area, and news about him had spread far and wide (Mark 1:28).

BIBLE CHUNK Read Luke 5:27–32

(27) After this, Jesus went out and saw a tax collector by the name of Levi sitting at his tax booth. "Follow me," Jesus said to him, (28) and Levi

got up, left everything and followed him.

(29) Then Levi held a great banquet for Jesus at his house, and a large crowd of tax collectors and others were eating with them. (30) But the Pharisees and the teachers of the law who belonged to their sect complained to his disciples, "Why do you eat and drink with tax collectors and 'sinners'?"

(31) Jesus answered them, "It is not the healthy who need a doctor, but the sick. (32) I have not come to call the righteous, but sinners to repentance."

STUFF TO KNOW In Matthew 9:9 Levi is identified as Matthew—yep, the guy who wrote the Bible book. So where does Jesus find Levi? And what does he say to him (verse 27)?

SIDELIGHT There's a Sunday school song that goes, "Zacchaeus was a wee little man. . . ." Like Zacchaeus, Levi was a tax collector. Because tax collectors worked for the Romans who occupied Israel and often scammed money for themselves, they were even less popular back in Bible times than they are today. The Pharisees put them on par with prostitutes and other big-time evildoers.

So how does Levi react to Jesus' invitation (verse 28)?

INSIGHT Jesus doesn't say, "Wanna hang out?" He speaks a command, expecting instant and absolute obedience. But he wasn't barking to strangers. He was calling people who had very likely become convinced they could trust him.

Right after Levi decides to follow Jesus, he calls a prayer service and only invites his new Christian friends, right? What's actually going on (verse 29)?

INSIGHT Instead of ditching his old friends, Levi invites them home. See how he's not hiding Jesus from people who might think he's uncool? And Jesus makes quick friends with these outcasts.

Who has a problem with Jesus? What's the big deal (verse 30)?

INSIGHT The Pharisees think Jesus is dining with swine. In their minds, they weren't just being picky. To them, eating with a sinner was nearly as bad as joining a sinner in an evil deed, and making friends with a sinner without a doubt made you evil. This is the first time the Pharisees publicly snipe at Jesus. In the last scene in Luke, they didn't even openly speak their thoughts (Luke 5:21). This time they pick on the disciples. Who do you suppose will get nailed next?

How does Jesus shut up his critics? Who does he say needs a doctor? What's Jesus mean by that (verse 31)?

INSIGHT The Bible is clear that no one is righteous (Romans 3:23). So Jesus is making his point with a sharp poke: As long as people think they're too good to need help, they'll stay spiritually sick and not even know it.

BIG QUESTIONS What do you see as the pros and cons of *you* following Jesus? Scribble some:

PROS	CONS

Looking at your lists, which is better? Following—or not?

SIDELIGHT When you hear the word *disciples,* you might think only of the twelve followers Jesus chose to be with him all the time (Luke 6:12–15). The name "disciple," though, applies to anyone who follows Jesus, including the larger band that trekked with Jesus as well as *you.* Jesus called his inner twelve "apostles," people he'd given a special job of spreading his message.

DEEP THOT Following Jesus—ditching wrong and sticking close to your Savior—isn't an optional part of the Christian life. In John 12:26 Jesus said, "Whoever serves me must follow me; and where I am, my servant also will be."

STICKY STUFF Luke 5:27–28 shows you how to do that following thing right.

ACT ON IT Spend some time thinking about things that keep you from following Jesus with total excitement.

DIG ON Look at some verses that tell you the cost of discipleship up front: Mark 8:34–38.

Talk About It • 2

EMPATHIZE: What's going on in your life?
ENCOURAGE: How are you doing with Jesus?
EQUIP: What one truth will you take home today?

- How do you react when you see someone acting like a hypocrite? (Study 6)
- What do you think about how Jesus cleared out the temple? (Study 6)
- If you could sneak up to Jesus and ask him a question without anyone hearing, what would you ask? (Study 7)
- Is getting to know God something you do because you *want* to—or because you *have* to? (Study 7)
- What cool stuff does John 3:16 promise to people who believe in him? How about John 3:18? (Study 7)
- What do you think of the Savior God promised to send? Did God have a good plan or what? (Study 8)
- What do you think of the fact that Jesus perfectly fulfilled all those Old Testament predictions? What does it prove about who he is? (Study 8)
- Why is the crowd in Jesus' hometown so mad? How would you have reacted to Jesus? (Study 9)
- When you try to live all-out for God, people might mock your spiritual intensity. How is the nastiness you might face like the hostility Jesus faced? (Study 9)
- How would you react if Jesus got right in your face and said, "Drop everything and follow me"? (Study 10)
- What are the pros and cons *you* listed of following Jesus? Which list wins? (Study 10)

PART 3

COACHING THE CLUELESS

11. Different—Not Dorky

The Sermon on the Mount

"Here's my next question," Becka announces to the girls in her small group Bible study. "So how do people know that you're Christians?" Long pause—then a list from the girls: "I suppose that I go to church." "Some of the T-shirts we wear." "I invite friends to youth events." "Go to camp." "We do socials." Becka wasn't satisfied. "I think there's more to it than that," she prods. "Those are just things you *do*. What's different about *you*?"

BRAIN DRAIN How can people tell that you follow Jesus?

FLASHBACK This is Jesus' first long preach in the Bible book of Matthew. While it's possible that Matthew pulled together teachings from different occasions—and Luke 6:20–49 makes it clear that Jesus taught on these topics more than once—he presents this Bible Chunk as a one-shot talk that must have left the disciples dazed. They were supposed to be radically different. But that didn't mean they had to be dorks.

BIBLE CHUNK Read Matthew 5:1–16

(1) Now when he saw the crowds, he went up on a mountainside and sat down. His disciples came to him, (2) and he began to teach them, saying:

(3) "Blessed are the poor in spirit,
for theirs is the kingdom of heaven.
(4) Blessed are those who mourn,

for they will be comforted.
(5) Blessed are the meek,
for they will inherit the earth.
(6) Blessed are those who hunger and thirst for righteousness,
for they will be filled.
(7) Blessed are the merciful,
for they will be shown mercy.
(8) Blessed are the pure in heart,
for they will see God.
(9) Blessed are the peacemakers,
for they will be called sons of God.
(10) Blessed are those who are persecuted because of righteousness,
for theirs is the kingdom of heaven.
(11) "Blessed are you when people insult you, persecute you and falsely
say all kinds of evil against you because of me. (12) Rejoice and be glad,
because great is your reward in heaven, for in the same way they persecuted the prophets who were before you.
(13) "You are the salt of the earth. But if the salt loses its saltiness, how can it be made salty again? It is no longer good for anything, except to be thrown out and trampled by men.
(14) "You are the light of the world. A city on a hill cannot be hidden.
(15) Neither do people light a lamp and put it under a bowl. Instead they put it on its stand, and it gives light to everyone in the house. (16) In the
same way, let your light shine before men, that they may see your good deeds and praise your Father in heaven."

STUFF TO KNOW Even though large crowds were listening, Jesus aims this radical preach at his followers. So what one word describes his followers best? (Hint: Spot it at the start of verses 3–11.)

DA'SCOOP "Blessed" sounds gaggy, but it's what you wanna be. "Blessed" actually means a big-time "happy." Yet it's not a temporary fluttery feeling. It's deep, unchanging peace.

Normally you don't picture people who are beaten down—poor in spirit, mourning, and meek—as incredibly happy. But what does God guarantee these folks (verses 3–5)?

DA'SCOOP The "poor in spirit" are the people who realize their total need for God. To be "meek" likewise means to have humility before God. Meekness remakes how you relate to people, but it doesn't make you a doormat for every cruel person in the world. To "mourn" isn't just any old sadness, but has at least partly to do with sorriness over sin.

So who else is happy (verses 6–10)?

SIDELIGHT In these "Beatitudes" Jesus isn't spewing commands and saying "Be like this!" You don't have to search out sorrow or volunteer to be bashed for your faith. Here's his point: If you truly know God, you'll catch both pain and blessedness.

Jesus says his followers are like two everyday items. So what good does it do the world for you to be "salt" (verse 13)? What's it like if you're "light" (verse 16)?

INSIGHT You know that salt makes stuff like chips and enchiladas taste swell. But back in Bible times salt was also an indispensable preservative. So if you're "salt," you keep the world from rotting—as long as you stay salty. To be "light" is to have a real faith that *naturally* shows up where people can see it (Matthew 5:14). Later in this sermon Jesus explains that people who pump up their religion in front of people just to be seen are losers (Matthew 6:1–4).

BIG QUESTIONS Do you think Jesus' expectations are for real? How come?

How are you "salt" and "light" to the people around you? Are you obnoxious about it?

DEEP THOT The Bible Chunk you read is just the start of how Jesus says his disciples stick out from their surroundings. He's got strong stuff to say about insults and hatred (5:21–26); sex (5:27–30); divorce (5:31–32); revenge (5:38–42); loving your enemies (5:43–48); generosity (6:1–4); prayer (6:5–15; 7:7–11); worry and wanting too much stuff (6:19–34); and being a spiritual snot (6:16–18; 7:1–6).

STICKY STUFF You're salt. Don't lose your saltiness (Matthew 5:13).

ACT ON IT Talk with your friends at church about good ways—and bad ways—you're different from everyone else around you.

DIG ON Dive into any one or more of those Bible Chunks in Deep Thot.

12. Off Your Butts

Jesus sends out his twelve disciples

"If you don't get going, this house won't get done," Jason barked. But gang-painting a house in the poor part of the city wasn't the thrill Jason's youth group expected. "It's hot," they whined in unison. The phrase "we thought this would be fun" barely made it out of their mouths when Jason raised his voice to just short of a scream. "But you said you wanted to do this!" he bellowed. And then he spit with frustration. "What does it take," he seethed, "to get you off your butts?"

BRAIN DRAIN What makes you serve: guilt that you're supposed to—or gladness for everything God has given you?

FLASHBACK In this Bible Chunk you'll see Jesus tell his twelve closest followers to do and say some potent stuff—the same miraculous deeds, in fact, that he's been doing. He isn't teasing. In other Bible Chunks Jesus promises that "anyone who has faith in me will do what I have been doing. He will do even greater things than these" (John 14:12). And when he gets done telling them *what* to do, he tells them *why* to do it.

BIBLE CHUNK Read Matthew 9:35–10:8

(9:35) Jesus went through all the towns and villages, teaching in their synagogues, preaching the good news of the kingdom and healing every disease and sickness. (9:36) When he saw the crowds, he had compassion on them, because they were harassed and helpless, like sheep without a shepherd. (9:37) Then he said to his disciples, "The harvest is plentiful but the workers are few. (9:38) Ask the Lord of the harvest, therefore, to send out workers into his harvest field."

(10:1) He called his twelve disciples to him and gave them authority to drive out evil spirits and to heal every disease and sickness.

(10:2) These are the names of the twelve apostles: first, Simon (who is called Peter) and his brother Andrew; James son of Zebedee, and his brother John; (10:3) Philip and Bartholomew; Thomas and Matthew the tax collector; James son of Alphaeus, and Thaddaeus; (10:4) Simon the Zealot and Judas Iscariot, who betrayed him.

(10:5) These twelve Jesus sent out with the following instructions: "Do not go among the Gentiles or enter any town of the Samaritans. (10:6) Go rather to the lost sheep of Israel. (10:7) As you go, preach this message: 'The kingdom of heaven is near.' (10:8) Heal the sick, raise the dead, cleanse those who have leprosy, drive out demons. Freely you have received, freely give."

STUFF TO KNOW What's Jesus doing as he's out on the town (verse 9:35)?

You can hear Jesus' gut churn as he ponders the crowds. What bugs him so badly (verse 9:36)?

Those crowds, Jesus declares, are ready to know God. What does Jesus tell his followers to do about it (verse 9:38)?

Hmmm . . . flip into the next study and it looks like the disciples become instant answers to their own prayers. Jesus sets them loose to do, um, pretty big stuff. Where do they get the mind-boggling power to do these deeds (verse 10:1)?

SIDELIGHT At this point the dozen disciples are to stay clear of the Gentiles (non-Jews) and Samaritans (despised cousins of the Jews). Later, Jesus sends his followers out with his message to *all* the world (Matthew 28:18–20; Acts 1:8).

For now, what are the disciples supposed to do (verses 10:7–8)?

Along with doing the powerful stuff Jesus *does*, what are they supposed to *say* (verse 10:7)?

SIDELIGHT Jesus knows that what his disciples say and do won't always be popular. He warns that they will be handed over to the religious rulers and flogged in the synagogues (Matthew 10:17).

And here's the biggie: *Why* are they supposed to do this stuff (last part of verse 10:8)?

BIG QUESTIONS What do you think of the assignment Jesus gave his budding spiritual students? Cool stuff or what?

What kinds of help have you gotten from God that would make you happily turn around and give help to others? Does that guarantee that serving will be easy?

SIDELIGHT Here's how Jesus wraps up his instructions—with words that cut to the heart of anyone contemplating following him: "Anyone who does not take his cross and follow me is not worthy of me. Whoever finds his life will lose it, and whoever loses his life for my sake will find it" (Matthew 10:38–39).

DEEP THOT When you follow Jesus, serving others isn't a *have to* thing. It's a *get to*. Still, doing God's deeds can be demanding, even to the point of death. This is the first time the cross is mentioned in the Bible book of Matthew. Jesus is letting his disciples in on the secret that following him is a costly, total commitment.

STICKY STUFF You can be the answer to your own prayers if you pray Matthew 9:38.

ACT ON IT Get your head together with your Christian friends and ask God together how you can do Jesus' deeds.

DIG ON Check out results of a larger group of disciples going out to minister in Luke 10:17–24.

13. Got Ears?

The parable of the sower

When Jesus wanted the world to hear his message, he didn't book cheapo middle-of-the-night airtime on local cable access. He went to where people were. He helped them. And the crowds flocked. Jesus knew, though, that people wouldn't connect with God if they were only wowed by miracles and didn't heed his words. Some days he doubted the crowds were paying attention (Matthew 11:16–24). And he told them so.

BRAIN DRAIN What kind of consequences do you face when you zone out and don't listen to something you're supposed to learn—say, at school?

FLASHBACK Jesus didn't always talk in straightforward statements like "For God so loved the world . . ." or "You are the salt. . . ." To make his point he also told stories pulled from everyday life. The main point of these "parables" was usually more important than the details. Often the point was hidden to anyone not tuned in to God. And sometimes the point was so hard to figure out that his closest disciples were clueless. So Jesus had to explain. . . .

BIBLE CHUNK Read Matthew 13:1–13, 18–23

(1) That same day Jesus went out of the house and sat by the lake.
(2) Such large crowds gathered around him that he got into a boat and sat
in it, while all the people stood on the shore. (3) Then he told them many

things in parables, saying: "A farmer went out to sow his seed. (4) As he was scattering the seed, some fell along the path, and the birds came and ate it up. (5) Some fell on rocky places, where it did not have much soil. It sprang up quickly, because the soil was shallow. (6) But when the sun came up, the plants were scorched, and they withered because they had no root. (7) Other seed fell among thorns, which grew up and choked the plants. (8) Still other seed fell on good soil, where it produced a crop—a hundred, sixty or thirty times what was sown. (9) He who has ears, let him hear."

(10) The disciples came to him and asked, "Why do you speak to the people in parables?"

(11) He replied, "The knowledge of the secrets of the kingdom of heaven has been given to you, but not to them. (12) Whoever has will be given more, and he will have an abundance. Whoever does not have, even what he has will be taken from him. (13) This is why I speak to them in parables. . . .

(18) "Listen then to what the parable of the sower means: (19) When anyone hears the message about the kingdom and does not understand it, the evil one comes and snatches away what was sown in his heart. This is the seed sown along the path. (20) The one who received the seed that fell on rocky places is the man who hears the word and at once receives it with joy. (21) But since he has no root, he lasts only a short time. When trouble or persecution comes because of the word, he quickly falls away. (22) The one who received the seed that fell among the thorns is the man who hears the word, but the worries of this life and the deceitfulness of wealth choke it, making it unfruitful. (23) But the one who received the seed that fell on good soil is the man who hears the word and understands it. He produces a crop, yielding a hundred, sixty or thirty times what was sown."

STUFF TO KNOW The Bible book of Matthew gives us five long talks Jesus aimed at the crowds—rather than the people he knew were committed to him. This Bible Chunk is part of the first, where "he told them many things in parables."

Explain in terms that city folk can understand what the farmer is doing (verse 3).

What happens to the seed that falls . . .

- along the path (verse 4)?

- in rocky places (verses 5–6)?

- among thorns (verse 7)?

- on good soil (verse 8)?

INSIGHT Here's where Jesus tells the disciples why he speaks in parables. It hides the point, Jesus says, from people who are already hardhearted toward God (Matthew 13:9–17).

So what's all this mean? What is the seed strewn "along the path" supposed to represent (verse 19)?

How 'bout the seed on the rocky soil? What makes it wither (verses 20–21)?

What chokes the seed in the thorny soil (verse 22)?

And whazzup with the good soil? Why does that seed succeed (verse 23)?

BIG QUESTIONS There's nothing wrong with the seed—the message Jesus brings. But the soil can be a problem. So what kind of soil are you? How do you know?

Jesus says that people without "ears" won't hear what he says (verse 9). How do you suppose you get ears?

DEEP THOT It's possible for you to be taught by people about God and never really listen. It's possible for you to go through the hard knocks of everyday life and overlook what God wants to teach you. And it's possible for you to lick at the message of the Bible and never actually swallow. If you have ears, *hear*.

STICKY STUFF Listen up like the good soil in Matthew 13:23.

ACT ON IT Talk to God. Tell him you want to be good soil.

DIG ON Keep reading on through half a dozen more parables in Matthew 13. You can also flip through a bunch in Luke 14–18. Many study Bibles also provide a complete list of these funky stories of Jesus.

14. Power Encounters

Jesus feeds 5,000

Jesus did more than preach and tell parables. He proved God's power. Take a peek at just a few of his miracles: He caused a paralyzed man to walk (Mark 2:3–12) . . . healed a man born blind (John 9:1) . . . brought an official's son back from the brink of death (John 4:46–54) . . . calmed a storm (Mark 4:37–41) . . . caused a miraculously huge catch of fish (Luke 5:4–11) . . . cast out a legion of demons and pointed them to a bunch of pigs (Mark 5:1–20) . . . raised a widow's son from the dead (John 11:1–44) . . . and healed countless others of physical illnesses and demonizations. The day-in-day-out ministry of Jesus was about *preaching, parables, and power*—all done for the sake of *people* to bring *praise* to God.

BRAIN DRAIN So of all the things Jesus did, which are you most wowed by?

FLASHBACK In this next Bible Chunk you see Jesus take a little bit of food and feed a huge mob. Some modern folks have a *had-to-be-there-to-eat-that* attitude toward believing a miracle actually took place, figuring that Jesus was such a nice guy that everyone whipped out their lunches and started sharing. But people who were there obviously knew something supernatural had happened, and this miracle sure didn't happen off in a corner where no one could see it—or criticize it. . . .

BIBLE CHUNK Read John 6:1–15

(1) Some time after this, Jesus crossed to the far shore of the Sea of Galilee (that is, the Sea of Tiberias), (2) and a great crowd of people fol-

lowed him because they saw the miraculous signs he had performed on the sick. (3) Then Jesus went up on a mountainside and sat down with his disciples. (4) The Jewish Passover Feast was near.

(5) When Jesus looked up and saw a great crowd coming toward him, he said to Philip, "Where shall we buy bread for these people to eat?" (6) He asked this only to test him, for he already had in mind what he was going to do.

(7) Philip answered him, "Eight months' wages would not buy enough bread for each one to have a bite!"

(8) Another of his disciples, Andrew, Simon Peter's brother, spoke up, (9) "Here is a boy with five small barley loaves and two small fish, but how far will they go among so many?"

(10) Jesus said, "Have the people sit down." There was plenty of grass in that place, and the men sat down, about five thousand of them. (11) Jesus then took the loaves, gave thanks, and distributed to those who were seated as much as they wanted. He did the same with the fish.

(12) When they had all had enough to eat, he said to his disciples, "Gather the pieces that are left over. Let nothing be wasted." (13) So they gathered them and filled twelve baskets with the pieces of the five barley loaves left over by those who had eaten.

(14) After the people saw the miraculous sign that Jesus did, they began to say, "Surely this is the Prophet who is to come into the world." (15) Jesus, knowing that they intended to come and make him king by force, withdrew again to a mountain by himself.

STUFF TO KNOW

They've got thousands of people to feed—and not a Taco Bell Chalupa in sight. What does Jesus ask Philip? Why is his question so absurd (verses 5–7)?

Jesus is toying with Philip's mind. But the disciples also sound a little out of their minds. Why would Andrew bring Jesus a little kid—with his Happy Meal-sized lunch (verse 9)?

So what happened when Jesus got his hands on that Happy Meal (verses 11–13)?

Exactly how many people ate (verse 10)?

Matthew 14:21 points out that this wasn't just an all-guy pig-out. Jesus provided women, children, and men not merely a snack but *lots* to eat. What did all those folks think about Jesus (verse 14)? And what did they want to do (verse 15)?

BIG QUESTIONS If you'd been invited to that big buffet lunch, what would you have thought about Jesus?

How would you act if Jesus miraculously dropped lunch on you every day? (Make that more concrete: How would you treat the human who packs your lunch every day? Big hint: Do you, for example, take her for granted?)

SIDELIGHT Jesus wanted the people to take home more than full tummies. He wanted them to digest *him*. In verse 51 Jesus said this: "I am the living bread that came down from heaven. If anyone eats of this bread, he will live forever. This bread is my flesh, which I will give for the life of the world." When the people heard this, they said what amounts to "Help! How can we eat his body?" Many of the people who had been on his side said, "Too hard! We can't swallow this!" (John 6:60). And get this: Many of his followers stopped following (John 6:66).

How would you feel about following Jesus if he never gave you anything but his friendship—now and for eternity?

DEEP THOT The people liked lunch. But many didn't like his lecture. When Jesus asked his twelve closest friends, "You do not want to leave too, do you?" Peter piped up for the rest: "Lord, to whom shall we go? You have the words of eternal life" (John 6:68).

STICKY STUFF Munch on John 6:26–27.

ACT ON IT Make a list of anything where you feel you won't follow God if he doesn't do ____________ for you. Tell God you're happy with him alone. And then eat your list. Well, probably just throw it away.

DIG ON Read more about Jesus' miracles. You can find a complete list in most study Bibles.

15. Galactic Roller Coasters

Jesus walks on the water

You knew you were in for heavy-duty worship sessions in heaven. But you were shocked when you spotted the class *God's Galactic Roller Coasters 101* in the catalog for the College of Creation Appreciation. When Jesus unveiled the first riding assignment—a shiny million-mile roller coaster that hung in the sky like a moon—most of your classmates gasped and mumbled about dropping the class. You figured Jesus must know what he's doing. But you still wondered if your new heavenly body would barf.

BRAIN DRAIN If Jesus built a galaxy-sized roller coaster, would you trust him enough to ride?

FLASHBACK John 6:15 hints that the thousands who had lunch with Jesus in that last Bible Chunk actually planned to put Jesus at the front of a political uprising. Jesus had something different on his mind. Post-miracle, he sends his disciples for a sail, dismisses the crowd, and gets away to pray. But up comes another surprise. During the "fourth watch of the night," between three and six in the morning, Jesus goes for a stroll to meet his disciples. Here's the surprise: The guys were in the middle of the Sea of Galilee.

BIBLE CHUNK Read Matthew 14:22–33

(22) Immediately Jesus made the disciples get into the boat and go on ahead of him to the other side, while he dismissed the crowd. (23) After

he had dismissed them, he went up on a mountainside by himself to pray. When evening came, he was there alone, (24) but the boat was already a considerable distance from land, buffeted by the waves because the wind was against it.

(25) During the fourth watch of the night Jesus went out to them, walking on the lake. (26) When the disciples saw him walking on the lake, they were terrified. "It's a ghost," they said, and cried out in fear.

(27) But Jesus immediately said to them: "Take courage! It is I. Don't be afraid."

(28) "Lord, if it's you," Peter replied, "tell me to come to you on the water."

(29) "Come," he said.

Then Peter got down out of the boat, walked on the water and came toward Jesus. (30) But when he saw the wind, he was afraid and, beginning to sink, cried out, "Lord, save me!"

(31) Immediately Jesus reached out his hand and caught him. "You of little faith," he said, "why did you doubt?"

(32) And when they climbed into the boat, the wind died down. (33) Then those who were in the boat worshiped him, saying, "Truly you are the Son of God."

STUFF TO KNOW Keep this point in mind as you ponder this passage: What's the weather like as the disciples row across the lake (verse 24)?

So what do the disciples think when they see Jesus walking on the waves (verse 26)?

INSIGHT Before you jump to conclude that the disciples were idiots overcome by ancient superstitions, ponder this: What would *you* think was walking at you on the water? You might suddenly wonder about ghosts too.

So how does Jesus calm down the weirded-out disciples (verse 27)?

Peter says, "Me too! Me too!" What does he want to try (verse 28)?

Peter's mom isn't around to say something like "Walking on the water is only funny until someone drowns." And what happens when Peter tries? Why (verse 30)?

What's the problem with Peter's water-walking (verse 31)?

Jesus saves Peter, and when they climb into the boat the winds stop. Hmm . . . how do the disciples react (verse 33)?

INSIGHT "Son of God" is a pretty huge thing to call Jesus. But Jesus must think the disciples don't fully get what they're saying, because he focuses on their *lack* of belief. Wait until you see his reaction when Peter tries out that title again in the next Bible Chunk.

BIG QUESTIONS Assuming you've signed the necessary legal forms to hold Jesus and the owners of the Sea of Galilee blameless should you be injured or killed in the attempt, would you have walked on the water? Why or why not?

INSIGHT Count how many times "the wind" is mentioned in this Bible Chunk and you realize that Jesus' disciples—several of them professional fishermen—felt endangered. Seeing something coming at them over the water makes them feel no safer. They only feel fine when Jesus climbs into the boat with them and the wind and the waves calm.

What does trust have to do with following Jesus wherever he commands you to go?

DEEP THOT Maybe you're sure you'd survive a million-mile coaster ride. But Jesus calls you into spiritual fun far beyond what you can stomach on your own—like walking on water. The only question is whether you'll take him up on his dare to trust him in every daring move of life. Whatever he asks you to do, he gives you the power to do.

STICKY STUFF Jesus asks a good question in Matthew 14:31. Do you have a good answer?

ACT ON IT If you have any doubts about Jesus' greatness, fill a bathtub with a foot of water and try to walk across the top.

DIG ON Read about Jesus calming a nasty full-blown storm in Matthew 8:23–27.

Talk About It • 3

EMPATHIZE: What's going on in your life?
ENCOURAGE: How are you doing with Jesus?
EQUIP: What one truth will you take home today?

- How can people tell that you follow Jesus? (Study 11)
- Does it sound like a good thing to be "blessed" by God? Why or why not? (Study 11)
- Do you think Jesus really expects you to live up to his teachings? How come? (Study 11)
- How are you "salt" and "light" to the people around you? Are you obnoxious about it? (Study 11)
- What do you think of the ministry assignment Jesus gave his budding spiritual students? Cool stuff or what? (Study 12)
- Does Jesus guarantee that following him will be easy? (Study 12)
- So what kind of soil are you? (Study 13)
- If you don't have "ears," how do you get them? (Study 13)
- Of all the powerful things Jesus did, which are you most wowed by? (Study 14)
- How would you feel about following Jesus if he never gave you anything but his friendship—now and for eternity? (Study 14)
- If Jesus built a galaxy-sized roller coaster, would you trust him enough to ride? (Study 15)
- What does trust have to do with following Jesus wherever he commands you to go? (Study 15)

PART 4

GROWING HIS FOLLOWERS

16. Who Do You Say I Am?

Peter's confession of Christ

Some people label the Jesus you see in the Bible a legend. But to do that you have to ignore points of Bible history that are highly reliable—biggie things like the acts and prophecies of God in the Old Testament; the facts of Jesus' life, death, and resurrection; and the explosive birth of the church. You'd also have to ignore facts about the Bible itself, since there's far more evidence for the accuracy of the Bible than for other histories from the way-back world. But it's not enough to have facts humming around in your head about who Jesus is. Jesus wants you to know him up close and personal. He wants you to know him for yourself.

BRAIN DRAIN If Jesus stood in front of you and said, "So who do you think I am?" what would you say?

FLASHBACK By the time this Bible Chunk rolls around, it's likely that Jesus has hung out with his disciples for nearly two years. They've witnessed his miracles. They've mulled his sermons. They've watched his kindness toward people everyone else considered scum. And now that they've seen all this, Jesus asks his closest followers a short, simple question.

BIBLE CHUNK Read Matthew 16:13–17, 21–28

(13) When Jesus came to the region of Caesarea Philippi, he asked his disciples, "Who do people say the Son of Man is?"

(14) They replied, "Some say John the Baptist; others say Elijah; and still

others, Jeremiah or one of the prophets."

(15) "But what about you?" he asked. "Who do you say I am?"

(16) Simon Peter answered, "You are the Christ, the Son of the living God."

(17) Jesus replied, "Blessed are you, Simon son of Jonah, for this was not revealed to you by man, but by my Father in heaven. . . ."

(21) From that time on Jesus began to explain to his disciples that he must go to Jerusalem and suffer many things at the hands of the elders, chief priests and teachers of the law, and that he must be killed and on the third day be raised to life.

(22) Peter took him aside and began to rebuke him. "Never, Lord!" he said. "This shall never happen to you!"

(23) Jesus turned and said to Peter, "Get behind me, Satan! You are a stumbling block to me; you do not have in mind the things of God, but the things of men."

(24) Then Jesus said to his disciples, "If anyone would come after me,
he must deny himself and take up his cross and follow me. (25) For whoever wants to save his life will lose it, but whoever loses his life for me will
find it. (26) What good will it be for a man if he gains the whole world, yet
forfeits his soul? Or what can a man give in exchange for his soul? (27) For
the Son of Man is going to come in his Father's glory with his angels, and
then he will reward each person according to what he has done. (28) I tell
you the truth, some who are standing here will not taste death before they
see the Son of Man coming in his kingdom."

STUFF TO KNOW Calling himself "the Son of Man," Jesus shoots a straightforward question at his disciples. What does he ask (verse 13)?

So what's the buzz about Jesus? What do the crowds say (verse 14)?

INSIGHT Some people argue that Jesus is John the Baptist—John back from the dead, that is, since he's been killed by Herod Antipas (Matthew 14:1–12). The rest think Jesus is a prophet announcing the Savior God has promised—but not the Savior himself.

And here's the most gargantuan question of the Bible: What does Jesus ask Peter (verse 15)?

Remember: Peter has been eyeballing Jesus more closely than anyone else on earth. And who does he say Jesus is (verse 16)?

INSIGHT The disciples no doubt had chatted about the true identity of Jesus. But Peter's words are a first-time, mind-blowing recognition of Jesus. Possibly speaking for the group, he bluntly says that Jesus is the chosen one come to rescue God's people. And Peter is starting to understand that Jesus is God.

Jesus pats Peter on the back big time, but all isn't well. Now that his herd knows who he is, Jesus breaks some bad news. What does he say is going to happen (verse 21)?

Peter isn't happy—and trying to be helpful, he protests Jesus' deadly prediction. And OUCH! If Peter aced that last test, he just bombed this one. What does Jesus blast back? Where does he say Peter's mission-killing attitude comes from (verse 23)?

INSIGHT Jesus scolds Peter for one simple reason: Peter is hindering God's plan for Jesus to die for the sins of humankind.

BIG QUESTIONS If you lived back in Bible times and had watched Jesus firsthand, what would you think about him?

That was then. This is now. So who do you say Jesus is?

DEEP THOT When you spot the disciples finally figuring out Jesus, you've reached one of the high points of the Bible. But it also means the ball of history is rolling—inescapably—down toward the cross: "From that time on Jesus began to explain to his disciples that he *must* go to Jerusalem and suffer many things at the hands of the elders, chief priests and teachers of the law, and that he *must* be killed. . . ." (Matthew 16:21, italics added). But Jesus also made a bigger promise. On the third day after his death he would rise again.

STICKY STUFF Matthew 16:16 is the answer to the most important question anyone could ever ask you.

ACT ON IT Tell someone what you think about Jesus.

DIG ON In this chunk you see Peter at his best—and worst. Here's some more of Peter struggling (Matthew 26:69–75) and growing (John 21:15–19).

17. Aunt Slobbers

The transfiguration

As you tiptoe through your cousin's wedding reception, you spot your aunt. Worse, Auntie Bess spots you. Your eyes meet hers. You're like a helpless baby deer locking looks with a mountain lion. She lunges through the crowd and pounces, pinching your left cheek and planting a car-wash-sized smooch on the right. "You look *soooo* grown-up in your wedding clothes," she slobbers. "And, I must say, you look *soooo* much like *my* side of the family."

BRAIN DRAIN What do you look like at your scrubbed-up best? And while you're at it, describe the weirdest thing your parents ever made you wear.

FLASHBACK The disciples are reaching huge conclusions about who Jesus is. But they've never seen him like they will in this Bible Chunk, displaying the splendor he had in heaven before being born as a baby on planet Earth (John 1:14; 17:5). They see Jesus shimmer with the bright shining glory of God. And just like the Father gave Jesus a boost at his baptism—the start of his ministry—this "transfiguration" comforts and confirms Jesus as he heads toward the cross.

BIBLE CHUNK Read Matthew 17:1–9

(1) After six days Jesus took with him Peter, James and John the brother of James, and led them up a high mountain by themselves. (2) There he was transfigured before them. His face shone like the sun, and his clothes

became as white as the light. (3) Just then there appeared before them Moses and Elijah, talking with Jesus.

(4) Peter said to Jesus, "Lord, it is good for us to be here. If you wish, I will put up three shelters—one for you, one for Moses and one for Elijah."

(5) While he was still speaking, a bright cloud enveloped them, and a voice from the cloud said, "This is my Son, whom I love; with him I am well pleased. Listen to him!"

(6) When the disciples heard this, they fell facedown to the ground, terrified. (7) But Jesus came and touched them. "Get up," he said. "Don't be afraid." (8) When they looked up, they saw no one except Jesus.

(9) As they were coming down the mountain, Jesus instructed them, "Don't tell anyone what you have seen, until the Son of Man has been raised from the dead."

STUFF TO KNOW Do the math: How many people head up the mountain with Jesus? Who? (verse 1)

INSIGHT You've seen crowds swarm Jesus. You also know that Jesus picked twelve people as his closest disciples. Here you see the inner three—the closest of the close. The same three show up with Jesus in a scene right before his death.

So what happens after Jesus and friends sprint up the mountain (verse 2)?

As if that isn't eerie enough, suddenly it's not four of them anymore. Who shows up next (verse 3)?

INSIGHT The word that describes the transfiguration of Jesus means "a change of inmost nature that may be outwardly visible." In the Old Testament Moses had glowed, but he only *reflected* God's glory (Exodus 34:29–30). Jesus shines from the inside out.

Peter blurts something strange. What does he want to do (verse 4)?

Maybe Peter wants to toss up some pup tents to make this experience last, but Mark 9:6 says he was so scared he didn't know what else to say. His suggestion slides by—and then something else happens. Who speaks? What does he say (verse 5)?

SIDELIGHT Sound familiar? Peek back at what the Father spoke at Jesus' baptism (Matthew 3:17).

And what happens at the end? Who freaks? Who disappears? Who's left to clean up after the party (verses 6–7)?

BIG QUESTIONS How would you react if you suddenly saw Jesus dripping with his heavenly glory?

You gotta wonder why Peter, James, and John hadn't fallen down with fright right at the start of this awestriking event. But Jesus comforts them—and tells them to keep what they'd seen under wraps until he had risen from the dead. So if the transfiguration is supposed to be a secret, why does Jesus bring his disciples with him?

INSIGHT Peter, James, and John see that Jesus is superior to the two biggest figures in Old Testament faith. They hear God declare him to be his Son. And as Jesus heads toward his crucifixion, they're reassured that Jesus is on the right path.

So does the transfiguration do anything for *your* faith in who Jesus is?

DEEP THOT For all that the disciples had figured out about Jesus, the transfiguration shows that there was even more to him than what they knew. It was time to hang on tight.

STICKY STUFF Matthew 17:2 tells you what Jesus looked like when God flipped on the lights.

ACT ON IT Check the verse in *Dig On*, then ask God to display his glory in you as you get to know him.

DIG ON Slide over to 2 Corinthians 3:18, which says that *you* reflect God's glory.

18. There's a Bad Odor

Jesus is the resurrection and life

Back in the Old Testament, the idea of life after death was hazy. By the time the New Testament age arrived, some Jews had a big-enough-to-fistfight-about-it belief in a post-death "resurrection" of God's people. Yet others sneered at the idea (Acts 23:6–10). In this Bible Chunk, Jesus is about to provide a explanation. Better yet, he's about to do a demonstration.

BRAIN DRAIN What do you expect will happen to you after you die?

FLASHBACK Yep, this Bible Chunk has the shortest verse in the Bible: "Jesus wept." It also contains one of the sassiest: " 'But, Lord,' said Martha, the sister of the dead man, 'by this time there is a bad odor, for he has been there four days.' " But it also relays one of the Bible's most significant: "Jesus said . . . 'I am the resurrection and the life . . . whoever lives and believes in me will never die.' " Read on.

BIBLE CHUNK Read John 11:17–44

(17) On his arrival, Jesus found that Lazarus had already been in the tomb for four days. (18) Bethany was less than two miles from Jerusalem, (19) and many Jews had come to Martha and Mary to comfort them in the loss of their brother. (20) When Martha heard that Jesus was coming, she went out to meet him, but Mary stayed at home.

(21)"Lord," Martha said to Jesus, "if you had been here, my brother would not have died. (22) But I know that even now God will give you whatever you ask."

(23) Jesus said to her, "Your brother will rise again."

(24) Martha answered, "I know he will rise again in the resurrection at the last day."

(25) Jesus said to her, "I am the resurrection and the life. He who believes in me will live, even though he dies; (26) and whoever lives and believes in me will never die. Do you believe this?"

(27) "Yes, Lord," she told him, "I believe that you are the Christ, the Son of God, who was to come into the world."

(28) And after she had said this, she went back and called her sister Mary aside. "The Teacher is here," she said, "and is asking for you." (29) When Mary heard this, she got up quickly and went to him. (30) Now Jesus had not yet entered the village, but was still at the place where Martha had met him. (31) When the Jews who had been with Mary in the house, comforting her, noticed how quickly she got up and went out, they followed her, supposing she was going to the tomb to mourn there.

(32) When Mary reached the place where Jesus was and saw him, she fell at his feet and said, "Lord, if you had been here, my brother would not have died."

(33) When Jesus saw her weeping, and the Jews who had come along with her also weeping, he was deeply moved in spirit and troubled. (34) "Where have you laid him?" he asked.

"Come and see, Lord," they replied.

(35) Jesus wept.

(36) Then the Jews said, "See how he loved him!"

(37) But some of them said, "Could not he who opened the eyes of the blind man have kept this man from dying?"

(38) Jesus, once more deeply moved, came to the tomb. It was a cave with a stone laid across the entrance. (39) "Take away the stone," he said.

"But, Lord," said Martha, the sister of the dead man, "by this time there is a bad odor, for he has been there four days."

(40) Then Jesus said, "Did I not tell you that if you believed, you would see the glory of God?"

(41) So they took away the stone. Then Jesus looked up and said, "Father, I thank you that you have heard me. (42) I knew that you always hear me, but I said this for the benefit of the people standing here, that they may believe that you sent me."

(43) When he had said this, Jesus called in a loud voice, "Lazarus, come out!" (44) The dead man came out, his hands and feet wrapped with strips of linen, and a cloth around his face.

Jesus said to them, "Take off the grave clothes and let him go."

STUFF TO KNOW

Jesus has been road-tripping. But

what's his friend Lazarus been doing (verse 17)? Who else is present when Jesus shows up (verse 19)?

Martha's got a heap of confidence in Jesus. She thinks he could have saved her brother if he'd just shown up a tad sooner. Even so, does it sound like Martha expects Jesus to yank Lazarus back to life (verses 22–24)?

INSIGHT Martha takes Jesus' words as a happy thought for her sad heart—that Jesus is reassuring her that Lazarus will rise at the end of time with everyone else. Jesus is trying to tell her what he's going to do *right now*.

What does Jesus take the opportunity to tell her (verses 25–26)?

Those are big words—unless Jesus can back them up. What does Jesus do to show his words are believable (verses 41–44)?

SIDELIGHT After praying to his Father, Jesus speaks to the dead man. That's odd. But the words were a sharp, straight command that can be read, "Lazarus! This way out!" as if Jesus is directing him out of a dismal dungeon. That's not odd. That's awe-striking.

BIG QUESTIONS What huge promise does Jesus make to you if you believe in him—one you'll want to take advantage of someday?

Answer the question Jesus put to Martha (verse 40): Do you believe him? Why or why not?

DEEP THOT Jesus once said that a time will come when all who are in their graves will hear his voice (John 5:28). In this Bible Chunk he claims he's the "resurrection and the life." He proves that point by raising Lazarus. He'll soon prove it again by rising from the dead himself. And he'll prove it once more when he pulls you out of the grave.

STICKY STUFF There's a good chance someone will someday read John 11:25–26 at your funeral.

ACT ON IT Talk with your parents or your pastor about a Christian you know who has died. What difference did it make that he or she could face death knowing Jesus is "the resurrection and the life"?

DIG ON Check out the victory chant in 1 Corinthians 15:55.

19. Revenge of the Rug Rats

Jesus blesses little kids

Unkind facts of adolescent life: Some teachers say you're brainless—and they do nothing more than baby-sit you until graduation. Lots of adults call you hopeless—and judge you by your hair, your clothes, your music, and your friends. Most sales clerks assume you're evil—and follow you around waiting for you to steal the store. A lot of adults won't take you seriously. God does. A lot of adults think you're clueless. God has a better opinion.

BRAIN DRAIN Do the adults in your life think you're capable of real spiritual growth? How do they show that—or not?

FLASHBACK Kids were a vital part of Old Testament faith. God told parents, for example, to make spiritual growth part of *everything* in children's lives: "Impress [these spiritual truths] on your children. Talk about them when you sit at home and when you walk along the road, when you lie down and when you get up" (Deuteronomy 6:7). Even so, in the culture of Jesus' time children counted for less than adults. Their role was to hush up and blend into the background. Jesus disagreed.

BIBLE CHUNK Read Matthew 19:13–15

(13) Then little children were brought to Jesus for him to place his hands on them and pray for them. But the disciples rebuked those who brought them.

(14) Jesus said, "Let the little children come to me, and do not hinder

them, for the kingdom of heaven belongs to such as these." (15) When he had placed his hands on them, he went on from there.

STUFF TO KNOW At the beginning of this Bible Chunk, who shows up at Jesus' feet? Why (verse 13)?

So how do the disciples react to what they see as the scurry of rug rats (verse 13)?

INSIGHT It wasn't strange for parents to bring children to a Jewish teacher or elder to be blessed with a touch on the head and a prayer. More unusual is the way the disciples square off with the people who bring their kids. The disciples maybe think Jesus has appointments to keep or important points to make—things they reckon more pressing than blessing kids.

How does Jesus respond to his disciples' uninviting attitude (verse 14)?

SIDELIGHT Mark 10:14 adds that Jesus is "indignant" or "very upset" with his guys. They aren't living up to the attitudes he's been modeling—or to the words Jesus spoke to them in Matthew 18:1–5. His disciples wondered what it took to be really great in God's eyes. Here's what he hammered home:

> (1) At that time the disciples came to Jesus and asked, "Who is the greatest in the kingdom of heaven?"
>
> (2) He called a little child and had him stand among them. (3) And he said: "I tell you the truth, unless you change and become

like little children, you will never enter the kingdom of heaven. (4) Therefore, whoever humbles himself like this child is the greatest in the kingdom of heaven. (5) And whoever welcomes a little child like this in my name welcomes me."

Them are pointed words: Become like a little child, or you lose.

Back to Matthew 19. Exactly what does Jesus say belongs to the kiddies (verse 14)?

INSIGHT Jesus isn't saying that people won't know God once they're old enough to vote, join the army, or buy beer. God's kingdom doesn't belong to children but to those who are *like* children. Jesus isn't applauding childish thinking (see Matthew 10:16) but childlike humility and trust.

SIDELIGHT Look at one more wise saying from Jesus to be sure of what he means about being childlike. In Matthew 11:25, Jesus notes that the spiritual snobs of his society are rejecting him—yet the people deemed spiritual rejects are lovin' him. And then he says this: "I praise you, Father, Lord of heaven and earth, because you have hidden these things from the wise and learned, and revealed them to little children." See it again? The people who know God best are the ones who depend on God and want to be taught. The upshot? If you think you've got it all figured out, you get left out.

BIG QUESTIONS Ponder the main point of what Jesus is saying. What qualities do children have that some adults lack?

Got any snotty attitudes you have to get rid of to nurture that child-like attitude God aims at? Details!

Do you think Jesus is *treating* you like a little kid by saying that you have to *trust* like a little kid? Why or why not?

How do you deal with oldsters who assume people your age aren't into spiritual things?

DEEP THOT It's hard work to bust up clodheaded thinking that says you're too young to know God well. But here's how you do it: "Don't let anyone look down on you because you are young, but set an example for the believers in speech, in life, in love, in faith and in purity" (1 Timothy 4:12).

STICKY STUFF You'll be truly smart if you sock Matthew 18:3 into your cerebrum.

ACT ON IT Do something today—without showing off—that demonstrates your spiritual maturity.

DIG ON Flip through the Bible books of 1 and 2 Timothy and ponder that Timothy was still young when Paul wrote to him.

20. Guess I'll Go Eat Worms

The triumphal entry

Your friends and neighbors had to admit your feat was worthy of the *Guinness Book of World Records*. Eating sixty-two night crawlers in thirty seconds stunned all of your fans. But their adoration didn't last forever. Maybe you overawed them when you offered to wash the worms down with a bowl of grubs and beetles. . . .

BRAIN DRAIN Suppose you did something incredibly great. How long do you think the cheers of the crowd would last?

FLASHBACK Just before this Bible Chunk, Jesus says he's headed to Jerusalem. Listen to the bone-crushing itinerary he lays out for his closest followers: "We are going up to Jerusalem, and the Son of Man will be betrayed to the chief priests and the teachers of the law. They will condemn him to death and will turn him over to the Gentiles to be mocked and flogged and crucified. On the third day he will be raised to life!" (Matthew 20:18–19). That's not a tour you'd find in a travel guide—yet it's what happened just half a dozen days later. It's not the end you'd expect when you see the royal welcome Jesus gets when he rides into town. . . .

BIBLE CHUNK Read Matthew 21:1–11

(1) As they approached Jerusalem and came to Bethphage on the Mount of Olives, Jesus sent two disciples, (2) saying to them, "Go to the

village ahead of you, and at once you will find a donkey tied there, with her colt by her. Untie them and bring them to me. (3) If anyone says anything to you, tell him that the Lord needs them, and he will send them right away."

(4) This took place to fulfill what was spoken through the prophet:

(5) "Say to the Daughter of Zion,
'See, your king comes to you,
gentle and riding on a donkey,
on a colt, the foal of a donkey.' "

(6) The disciples went and did as Jesus had instructed them. (7) They brought the donkey and the colt, placed their cloaks on them, and Jesus sat on them. (8) A very large crowd spread their cloaks on the road, while others cut branches from the trees and spread them on the road. (9) The crowds that went ahead of him and those that followed shouted,

"Hosanna to the Son of David!"
"Blessed is he who comes in the name of the Lord!"
"Hosanna in the highest!"

(10) When Jesus entered Jerusalem, the whole city was stirred and asked, "Who is this?"

(11) The crowds answered, "This is Jesus, the prophet from Nazareth in Galilee."

STUFF TO KNOW What does Jesus tell his followers to fetch (verse 2)?

SIDELIGHT Don't picture Jesus on a pony ride at a county fair. Jesus purposely rides into town not on a horse fitted for battle but on a symbol of peace. (He gets to ride a war horse when he returns to earth as king in Revelation 19:11–21.) His picking a colt was prophesied hundreds of years before in Zechariah 9:9.

How are the disciples supposed to find that rent-a-burro (verse 2)?

INSIGHT It's a mistake to brush aside obviously supernatural events in the Bible. But you don't need to see a big wow that isn't there. If you've been waving palm branches in Sunday school parades since you were little, you might have assumed Jesus supernaturally knew the location of the animal—and that its owners surrendered the colt in awe. The Bible doesn't say Jesus had a wooly revelation. He might have had a reservation.

Why is everyone ditching their *cloaks*—their old-time coats (verses 6–7)?

INSIGHT Laying coats and palm branches on the road is the Bible-era equivalent of rolling out a royal red carpet.

What do the people shout as Jesus rides by (verse 9)?

DA'SCOOP Look at these one by one: "Hosanna" is a shout of praise. "Son of David" recognizes the kingship of Jesus and his birth in the bloodline of David, Israel's greatest Old Testament king. "Blessed is he who comes in the name of the Lord," quotes Psalm 118:26, recognizing Jesus was sent by God. "Hosanna in the highest!" declares that everyone in heaven should sing praise to Jesus.

So how big of a commotion does the arrival of Jesus stir up (verses 10–11)?

BIG QUESTIONS Suppose Jesus was coming to your town. How ready would you be to toss your jacket in the road to let a donkey walk on it?

What would inspire you to show such a heap of respect?

DEEP THOT The Bible doesn't say that every person in this crowd turned on Jesus less than a week later and screamed for his death. It's clear that the religious leaders led the charge against Jesus, with help from dishonest thugs (Matthew 26:59). But Jesus wept as he entered Jerusalem, because the city as a whole didn't want the peace he offered (Luke 19:42). He must have known how quickly the cheers would turn to jeers.

STICKY STUFF Put some praise in your mouth. Memorize Matthew 21:9.

ACT ON IT Spend some time telling Jesus you think he's great.

DIG ON Flip to Luke 19:39–40 to read Jesus' answer to the Pharisees who didn't like him accepting the praises of the people.

Talk About It • 4

EMPATHIZE: What's going on in your life?
ENCOURAGE: How are you doing with Jesus?
EQUIP: What one truth will you take home today?

- If Jesus stood in front of you and said, "So who do you think I am?" what would you say? (Study 16)
- Who did the crowds say Jesus is? (Study 16)
- Who does Peter say Jesus is? Who do *you* say Jesus is? (Study 16)
- What do you look like at your scrubbed-up best? What's the weirdest thing your parents have ever made you wear? (Study 17)
- How would you react if you suddenly saw Jesus dripping with heavenly glory? (Study 17)
- What does the transfiguration do for your faith in who Jesus is? (Study 17)
- What do you expect will happen to you after you die? (Study 18)
- What life-and-death promise does Jesus make to you if you believe in him? Do you believe him? (Study 18)
- Do the adults in your life think you're capable of real spiritual growth? How do they show that—or not? (Study 19)
- How do you deal with oldsters who don't think you're into spiritual things? (Study 19)
- Why did the crowd cheer for Jesus? Why would people turn on him just a week later? (Study 20)

PART 5

POINTING US HOME

21. More Than a Meal

The last supper

When Steffi visited her friend's church she got a hunk of tasty bread and a sip of grape juice for communion. She thought it was cool her own church had 100% genuine wine—but she hated its weird paper-thin wafers. And one Sunday as a wafer welded itself to the roof of her mouth—and she panicked that it might be stuck there for the rest of her life—and she had to stick a finger up there to pick it loose—as she walked back to her seat, with the whole church watching—she wondered who thunk up this whole communion thing.

BRAIN DRAIN What does "communion" or "the Lord's Supper" mean to you?

FLASHBACK A ritual does no good without a reason. And the giant purpose of what Christians call "communion," "the Lord's Supper," or "the Eucharist" is *remembering Jesus' death on our behalf*. History note for this Bible Chunk: The "Passover" commemorates God's "passing over" Israelite slaves during a night of death that struck the firstborn of Egypt (Exodus 12:11). The "Feast of Unleavened Bread" celebrates God's setting the Israelites free from slavery (Exodus 12:17).

BIBLE CHUNK Read Matthew 26:17–30

(17) On the first day of the Feast of Unleavened Bread, the disciples came to Jesus and asked, "Where do you want us to make preparations for you to eat the Passover?"

(18) He replied, "Go into the city to a certain man and tell him, 'The Teacher says: My appointed time is near. I am going to celebrate the Passover with my disciples at your house.' " (19) So the disciples did as Jesus had directed them and prepared the Passover.

(20) When evening came, Jesus was reclining at the table with the Twelve. (21) And while they were eating, he said, "I tell you the truth, one of you will betray me."

(22) They were very sad and began to say to him one after the other, "Surely not I, Lord?"

(23) Jesus replied, "The one who has dipped his hand into the bowl with me will betray me. (24) The Son of Man will go just as it is written about him. But woe to that man who betrays the Son of Man! It would be better for him if he had not been born."

(25) Then Judas, the one who would betray him, said, "Surely not I, Rabbi?"

Jesus answered, "Yes, it is you."

(26) While they were eating, Jesus took bread, gave thanks and broke it, and gave it to his disciples, saying, "Take and eat; this is my body."

(27) Then he took the cup, gave thanks and offered it to them, saying, "Drink from it, all of you. (28) This is my blood of the covenant, which is poured out for many for the forgiveness of sins. (29) I tell you, I will not drink of this fruit of the vine from now on until that day when I drink it anew with you in my Father's kingdom."

(30) When they had sung a hymn, they went out to the Mount of Olives.

STUFF TO KNOW As this scene starts, what are Jesus and the disciples getting ready to do (verses 17–20)?

INSIGHT "Reclining at the table" sounds wildly casual, like plopping down with snacks on the family room floor. It actually was the usual way of dining.

What does Jesus say will happen soon? Who will do the evil deed (verses 21–25)?

SIDELIGHT Jesus' prediction comes true when his disciple Judas turns him over to the Jewish priests and elders for thirty pieces of silver (Matthew 26:47–56). When Judas realizes Jesus will die because of his betrayal, he is "seized with remorse" and hangs himself (Matthew 27:1–10).

The next thing Jesus does is a huge picture of the death he'll soon die. What does he say about the bread (verse 26)?

What does Jesus say about the cup of wine? What will it accomplish (verses 27–30)?

INSIGHT Remember how John the Baptist had called Jesus "the Lamb of God, who takes away the sin of the world" (John 1:29)? And Passover was the once-a-year feast that recalled how the blood of a lamb, splashed on doorjambs, protected Israelites from God's deadly wrath. Jesus gives the Passover meal another meaning—making it a picture of the sacrifice he was about to make. This time it would be the blood of Jesus that would spare people from God's anger over sin—and his blood would be God's unbreakable promise of forgiveness. In Luke 22:19 Jesus tells his followers to repeat this meal to remember him.

BIG QUESTIONS Does your church allow you to take part in the Lord's Supper? What have you been told it means?

DA'SCOOP Churches give different names to this sacred meal—names that hint at its deep, many-sided meaning. "The

Lord's Supper" is a straightforward name Paul used (1 Corinthians 11:20). "Communion" highlights the togetherness of the meal, that it's done "in common." And "Eucharist" is from a Greek word that means "to give thanks," emphasizing thankfulness for Jesus' death.

The Bible says we should think about our sins and the price Jesus paid for them before we take communion (1 Corinthians 11:28). What do you do to get ready for this more-than-merely-munching experience? What do you want to do differently to get set?

DEEP THOT Celebrating the Lord's Supper is a great habit. But the meal easily loses its meaning. Ponder this as you prepare: Eating the bread and drinking from the cup is saying "yes" to Jesus, whose body was broken and whose blood was shed for you—all so your sins could be forgiven.

STICKY STUFF Jesus tells us what his supper means in Matthew 26:26–28.

ACT ON IT Ask your parents or your pastor what this meal means. Why is it something you still celebrate?

DIG ON Read what Paul had to say about the Lord's Supper in 1 Corinthians 11:23–26.

22. Not Guilty

Jesus' trial

Follow this action: After Jesus shared the first Lord's Supper with his disciples, he took his three closest followers—Peter, James, and John—and went to the Garden of Gethsemane to pray. He knew he was about to become the sacrifice for our total sins—the brunt of God's wrath. Jesus wondered if it was possible for him to save the world some other way, but he yielded to God's plan (Matthew 26:36–46). And as he finished praying, armed guards aided by Judas arrested him (Matthew 26:47–56).

BRAIN DRAIN Imagine you're Jesus. You're under arrest. You're headed to a death on the cross too agonizing for words. And you've done nothing wrong. How would you feel?

FLASHBACK After his arrest, Jesus was questioned by Caiaphas, the Jewish high priest. Asked straight-up if he was the Messiah, God's Son, Jesus said "yes" (Matthew 26:64). Caiaphas declared Jesus guilty of blasphemy—wickedly speaking against God. The religious leaders spit in his face and struck him with their fists (Matthew 26:67). And then came these chilling words: "All the chief priests and the elders of the people came to the decision to put Jesus to death. They bound him, led him away and handed him over to Pilate, the governor" (Matthew 27:1–2). Here's what happened as Jesus stood before Pilate.

BIBLE CHUNK Read John 18:28–40

(28) Then the Jews led Jesus from Caiaphas to the palace of the Roman governor. By now it was early morning, and to avoid ceremonial unclean-

ness the Jews did not enter the palace; they wanted to be able to eat the Passover. (29) So Pilate came out to them and asked, "What charges are you bringing against this man?"

(30) "If he were not a criminal," they replied, "we would not have handed him over to you."

(31) Pilate said, "Take him yourselves and judge him by your own law."

"But we have no right to execute anyone," the Jews objected. (32) This happened so that the words Jesus had spoken indicating the kind of death he was going to die would be fulfilled.

(33) Pilate then went back inside the palace, summoned Jesus and asked him, "Are you the king of the Jews?"

(34) "Is that your own idea," Jesus asked, "or did others talk to you about me?"

(35) "Am I a Jew?" Pilate replied. "It was your people and your chief priests who handed you over to me. What is it you have done?"

(36) Jesus said, "My kingdom is not of this world. If it were, my servants would fight to prevent my arrest by the Jews. But now my kingdom is from another place."

(37) "You are a king, then!" said Pilate.

Jesus answered, "You are right in saying I am a king. In fact, for this reason I was born, and for this I came into the world, to testify to the truth. Everyone on the side of truth listens to me."

(38) "What is truth?" Pilate asked. With this he went out again to the Jews and said, "I find no basis for a charge against him. (39) But it is your custom for me to release to you one prisoner at the time of the Passover. Do you want me to release 'the king of the Jews'?"

(40) They shouted back, "No, not him! Give us Barabbas!" Now Barabbas had taken part in a rebellion.

STUFF TO KNOW Do you catch the religious leaders' concern as they take Jesus to stand trial before Pilate, the Roman governor of the region? Entering the home of a non-Jew would make these leaders religiously unclean—and unable to take part in the rest of the Feast of Unleavened Bread. But Pilate isn't a Jew. What does he want to know from them (verse 29)?

The priests sound irritated with Pilate. Why? What does he tell them to do (verses 30–31)?

Pilate's idea doesn't satisfy Jesus' accusers. How come (verse 31)?

INSIGHT The religious leaders wanted Jesus dead—and fast. Only the Romans had the authority to crucify him.

Jesus boldly says what kind of king he came to be. What does he say (verses 36–37)?

Does Pilate find Jesus guilty—or not (verses 38)? What deal does he offer the religious leaders (verse 39)?

INSIGHT The Romans had a tradition of releasing a jailed criminal in recognition of the Passover. Pilate offers Jesus. His accusers want Barabbas, a notorious prisoner (Matthew 27:16).

BIG QUESTIONS How solid do the charges against Jesus sound?

Why would the religious leaders be so eager to kill Jesus?

Do you think Pilate dug hard to get at the truth about Jesus? How do you know from what he did? From what he said?

DEEP THOT Pilate's wife had a bad feeling about killing an innocent man, and she warned her husband to have nothing to do with Jesus (Matthew 27:19). John 19 says that Pilate had Jesus severely whipped, and soldiers pressed a crown of thorns onto his head and mockingly clothed him in a royal robe. Even though Pilate could find no fault in Jesus, he caved in to the shouts of the religious leaders for his death. And, says John 19:16, "Finally Pilate handed him over to them to be crucified."

STICKY STUFF John 18:37 tells what kind of king Jesus is.

ACT ON IT You no doubt know all about the Easter bunny. Ask around your church about what you do during the Easter season to remember the harsh stuff that happened to Jesus.

DIG ON Read more about Jesus' trial before Pilate in Luke 22:66–23:25. You can see Pilate's final decision in John 19:1–16.

23. Paying the Price

The crucifixion of Jesus

God said through the Old Testament prophet Isaiah that the Savior of the world would be "wounded for the wrong we did" and "crushed for the evil we did" (Isaiah 53:5 NCV). Here's the weird part: Not only did Jesus fulfill this prophecy—and all the other Old Testament predictions about the Savior—but he knew they pointed to him. You've seen how Jesus predicted his death. He had peered into the scary darkness. And now the darkness swallows him.

BRAIN DRAIN Are the wrong things you do bad enough that you should pay for them in some ultimate, cosmic way? Why or why not?

FLASHBACK The Bible says that all sin is so wrong—such a grotesque offense against God and goodness—that it earns the death penalty. Not frying in an electric chair or taking bullets from a firing squad, but an even uglier end: spiritual separation from God. Romans 6:23 describes it like this: "When people sin, they earn what sin pays—death. But God gives us a free gift—life forever in Christ Jesus our Lord" (NCV). If you have any doubts about the badness of sin, Jesus' horrid death shows the cost of your crimes.

BIBLE CHUNK Read Luke 23:32–49

(32) Two other men, both criminals, were also led out with him to be executed. (33) When they came to the place called the Skull, there they crucified him, along with the criminals—one on his right, the other on his

left. (34) Jesus said, "Father, forgive them, for they do not know what they are doing." And they divided up his clothes by casting lots.

(35) The people stood watching, and the rulers even sneered at him. They said, "He saved others; let him save himself if he is the Christ of God, the Chosen One."

(36) The soldiers also came up and mocked him. They offered him wine vinegar (37) and said, "If you are the king of the Jews, save yourself."

(38) There was a written notice above him, which read: THIS IS THE KING OF THE JEWS.

(39) One of the criminals who hung there hurled insults at him: "Aren't you the Christ? Save yourself and us!"

(40) But the other criminal rebuked him. "Don't you fear God," he said, "since you are under the same sentence? (41) We are punished justly, for we are getting what our deeds deserve. But this man has done nothing wrong."

(42) Then he said, "Jesus, remember me when you come into your kingdom."

(43) Jesus answered him, "I tell you the truth, today you will be with me in paradise."

(44) It was now about the sixth hour, and darkness came over the whole land until the ninth hour, (45) for the sun stopped shining. And the curtain of the temple was torn in two. (46) Jesus called out with a loud voice, "Father, into your hands I commit my spirit." When he had said this, he breathed his last.

(47) The centurion, seeing what had happened, praised God and said, "Surely this was a righteous man." (48) When all the people who had gathered to witness this sight saw what took place, they beat their breasts and went away. (49) But all those who knew him, including the women who had followed him from Galilee, stood at a distance, watching these things.

STUFF TO KNOW

Who was executed alongside Jesus (verse 32)?

What is Jesus' attitude toward his executioners (verse 34)?

INSIGHT Crucifixion was the cruelest punishment possible at the time of Jesus, a penalty saved for the most vile criminals of the Roman Empire. Victims were whipped down to the bone, stripped naked, then spiked by their hands and feet to a wood cross. Death came from starvation, exhaustion, or suffocation.

So how does one of the criminals slam Jesus (verse 39)? What does the other criminal shoot back (verses 41–42)?

INSIGHT Luke rattles off a couple key details: The darkness that covers the land—during midafternoon, mind you—is a sign of God's judgment. The veil that tears was meant to keep people out of the holiest place in the temple—and its tearing shows how Jesus ripped open the way to God (Hebrews 10:19–22).

A swarm of people watch Jesus die. What do they conclude about him (verses 47–49)?

BIG QUESTIONS Do you think Jesus was guilty of anything?

So why do you think Jesus died?

SIDELIGHT God couldn't be good and let evil run rampant. Sin couldn't be allowed to slip by. Humankind had a price to pay for evil. But Jesus did a one-of-a-kind loving thing: He stepped in and took the penalty we deserved so that our sins could be wiped clean. First Peter 3:18 says "Christ . . . died for our sins once for all time. He never sinned, but he died for sinners that he might bring us safely home to God" (NCV). He became that sacrificial Lamb of God who "takes away the sin of the world" (John 1:29).

You've heard that Jesus died for people's sins. Do you think he died for *yours*? What do you suppose that means?

DEEP THOUGHT Jesus the Son of God suffered in your place. He took the penalty for the wrongs of the whole human race—and that means he died for the wrongs you've done.

STICKY STUFF Luke 23:33–34 tells the story of Jesus' love for you.

ACT ON IT Ask some friends who wear crosses what that symbol means to them. Do their explanations at all resemble what Jesus suffered?

DIG ON Do a double take. Reread the Bible Chunk above, this time pondering the fact that it was *your* sins paid for on the cross.

24. Back From the Dead

The Resurrection

The Bible is brutally honest. It's up-front that if Jesus didn't rise up from the dead, Christians are due for a huge pity party. How come? If Jesus didn't come back from the dead, the Bible says, then (1) nothing has put us right with God; (2) we have no reason to think we will rise to eternal life; and (3) our faith is built on a fraud (1 Corinthians 15:19). It's true: The whole Christian faith hangs on the fact of the Resurrection. But here's the Good News: The Resurrection is real.

BRAIN DRAIN Does it matter to you if Jesus really rose from the dead? Why or why not?

FLASHBACK If someone wanted to prove to you that he was really God come to earth "in the flesh," then rising from the dead tops the wowser list. After his death was certified with a spear thrust into his side (John 19:34), Jesus was laid in the tomb of a wealthy secret follower (John 19:38) and sealed inside with an enormous stone (Matthew 27:60). Despite a crowd of guards keeping watch over the grave (Matthew 28:11–15), Jesus didn't stay in the tomb for long. Fact is, Jesus was "declared with power to be the Son of God by his resurrection from the dead" (Romans 1:4). In this Bible Chunk, Mary Magdalene—one of Jesus' closest followers—discovers Jesus has waved buh-bye to the grave. And he shows up to say hello to her.

BIBLE CHUNK Read John 20:1–18

(1) Early on the first day of the week, while it was still dark, Mary Magdalene went to the tomb and saw that the stone had been removed from the entrance. (2) So she came running to Simon Peter and the other disciple, the one Jesus loved, and said, "They have taken the Lord out of the tomb, and we don't know where they have put him!"

(3) So Peter and the other disciple started for the tomb. (4) Both were running, but the other disciple outran Peter and reached the tomb first. (5) He bent over and looked in at the strips of linen lying there but did not go in. (6) Then Simon Peter, who was behind him, arrived and went into the tomb. He saw the strips of linen lying there, (7) as well as the burial cloth that had been around Jesus' head. The cloth was folded up by itself, separate from the linen. (8) Finally the other disciple, who had reached the tomb first, also went inside. He saw and believed. (9) (They still did not understand from Scripture that Jesus had to rise from the dead.)

(10) Then the disciples went back to their homes, (11) but Mary stood outside the tomb crying. As she wept, she bent over to look into the tomb (12) and saw two angels in white, seated where Jesus' body had been, one at the head and the other at the foot.

(13) They asked her, "Woman, why are you crying?"

"They have taken my Lord away," she said, "and I don't know where they have put him." (14) At this, she turned around and saw Jesus standing there, but she did not realize that it was Jesus.

(15) "Woman," he said, "why are you crying? Who is it you are looking for?"

Thinking he was the gardener, she said, "Sir, if you have carried him away, tell me where you have put him, and I will get him."

(16) Jesus said to her, "Mary."

She turned toward him and cried out in Aramaic, "Rabboni!" (which means Teacher).

(17) Jesus said, "Do not hold on to me, for I have not yet returned to the Father. Go instead to my brothers and tell them, 'I am returning to my Father and your Father, to my God and your God.' "

(18) Mary Magdalene went to the disciples with the news: "I have seen the Lord!" And she told them that he had said these things to her.

STUFF TO KNOW Why is Mary so upset so early in the morning (verses 1–2)?

What has happened when Peter and the "other disciple"—John—get to the tomb (verses 6–8)?

INSIGHT At this point, John believes Jesus is *gone*. He doesn't realize Jesus has *risen*. He figures that out a few verses later (John 20:19–25).

What cures Mary's crying (verses 11–16)?

Jesus tells Mary to do something. What (verses 17–18)?

SIDELIGHT Jesus' appearance at the empty tomb is only the first of many post-grave encores:

- That same day Jesus appeared to two travelers (Luke 24:13–32), to Peter in Jerusalem (Luke 24:34), and to ten of the disciples—all but Thomas (John 20:19–25).
- A week later he showed up for all of the disciples, including Thomas, who had doubted that Jesus was really alive (John 20:26–31).
- Before Jesus headed to heaven forty days later (Luke 24:44–49), he appeared to seven (John 21:1–23) and eleven of his disciples (Matthew 28:16–20), to James (1 Corinthians 15:7), and to more than five hundred of his followers (1 Corinthians 15:6).

BIG QUESTIONS How does Jesus' rising from the dead prove to you he is who he claims to be—God in the flesh and Savior of the world?

What would you say to someone who argued that dead people stay dead—so Jesus' resurrection must be a hoax?

DEEP THOT Jesus told his followers that they were his witnesses—and that they would tell the world about him, starting in their hometown and extending to all nations. And at the end of his post-resurrection time on planet Earth, Jesus was "taken up into heaven," but not before vowing to return. More on that next time.

STICKY STUFF Share Mary's surprise and memorize John 20:18.

ACT ON IT If you have a hard time swallowing the real-life resurrection of Jesus, check out Josh McDowell's books *More Than a Carpenter* or *Don't Check Your Brains at the Door*.

DIG ON Check out the list of Jesus' back-from-the-dead appearances in 1 Corinthians 15:1–8.

25. The One Way Home

Jesus is the way, truth, and life

The Bible reports that forty days after his resurrection, Jesus ascended to heaven. He was "taken up" as his followers watched, "and a cloud hid him from their sight" (Acts 1:9–11). But Jesus didn't jet off to Disney World to celebrate his victory. He'd come to Earth on a mission, and "after he had provided purification for sins, he sat down at the right hand of the Majesty in heaven" (Hebrews 1:3). He's now back in the control center of the universe, forever on your side, living proof that your sins are forgiven (1 John 2:1–2). And—get this—he's promised he'll return. But He's not just swooping in for a visit. He's coming back to get you.

BRAIN DRAIN Jesus walked around in Israel two thousand years ago doing mind-boggling deeds. So why is it important to you that he's alive and well—not just another dead religious hero?

FLASHBACK The chapter number on this Bible Chunk looks like it's diving way back to the middle of Jesus' life. But it's only backing up a few days in the Bible's plot line. Jesus has predicted his betrayal by Judas (John 13:18–30). He's told his disciples he is going away (John 13:33). And he's also just revealed that Peter—one of those three closest friends and followers—will deny him not just once, but three times (John 13:38). The disciples are shaking. And here's how Jesus settles them down.

PUT YOUR LIFE ON THE RIGHT PATH

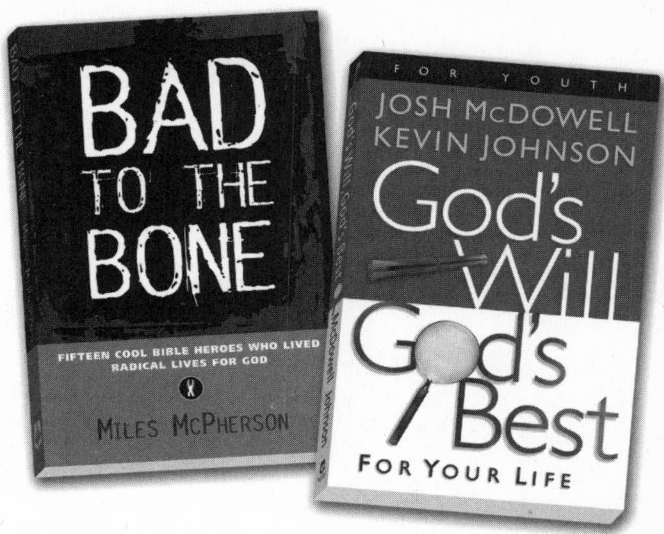

Understanding God's Will for Your Life

Happiness, a good career, good friends, and closeness with God are desires of everyone's heart. This book explains that God also desires to give these things to you—He even promises a specific plan for you to experience each of them. There's no catch, but there is a condition, a condition you can't afford to miss!

God's Will, God's Best
by Josh McDowell and Kevin Johnson

Life Lessons From Young Bible Heroes

Young Bible heroes like Daniel, Esther, and Josiah weren't afraid to go against the crowd. No matter what, they didn't back down from God's calling. They were committed to him all the way down to the bone, and God used them in supernatural ways. Want this for your life. Let this devotional rock you to the core!

Bad to the Bone by Miles McPherson

www.bethanyhouse.com

THANKS FOR PICKING A BETHANY BOOK

Bethany House Publishers is part of Bethany Fellowship International, a group of Christians who want to reach the world with God's Good News about Jesus by starting churches, printing Christian books, and caring for the poor. Bethany College of Missions is a school that trains missionaries.

If you would like to know more about what we do, please write:

Bethany Fellowship International
6820 Auto Club Road
Minneapolis, MN 55438 USA

SEE JESUS 5

Believing in Jesus

John 1:12

Yet to all who received him, to those who believed in his name, he gave the right to become children of God.

SEE JESUS 6

Jesus cleans out the temple

John 2:17 (NLT)

Then his disciples remembered this prophecy from the Scriptures: "Passion for God's house burns within me."

SEE JESUS 7

God wants to know you

John 3:16

"For God so loved the world that he gave his one and only Son, that whoever believes in him shall not perish but have eternal life."

SEE JESUS 8

Jesus fulfills prophecy

Luke 4:18–19

"The Spirit of the Lord is on me, because he has anointed me to preach good news to the poor. He has sent me to proclaim freedom for the prisoners and recovery of sight for the blind, to release the oppressed, to proclaim the year of the Lord's favor."

SEE JESUS 1

The Arrival of Jesus

Matthew 2:11

On coming to the house, they saw the child with his mother Mary, and they bowed down and worshiped him. Then they opened their treasures and presented him with gifts of gold and of incense and of myrrh.

SEE JESUS 2

When Jesus was your age

Luke 2:52

And Jesus grew in wisdom and stature, and in favor with God and men.

SEE JESUS 3

John the Baptist prepares the way for Jesus

Matthew 3:17

And a voice from heaven said, "This is my Son, whom I love; with him I am well pleased."

SEE JESUS 4

The temptation of Jesus

Matthew 4:4

Jesus answered, "It is written: 'Man does not live on bread alone, but on every word that comes from the mouth of God.' "

SEE JESUS 13

The parable of the sower

Matthew 13:23

"But the one who received the seed that fell on good soil is the man who hears the word and understands it. He produces a crop, yielding a hundred, sixty or thirty times what was sown."

SEE JESUS 14

Jesus feeds 5,000

John 6:26–27

Jesus answered, "I tell you the truth, you are looking for me, not because you saw miraculous signs but because you ate the loaves and had your fill. Do not work for food that spoils, but for food that endures to eternal life, which the Son of Man will give you."

SEE JESUS 15

Jesus walks on the water

Matthew 14:31

Immediately Jesus reached out his hand and caught him. "You of little faith," he said, "why did you doubt?"

SEE JESUS 16

Peter's confession of Christ

Matthew 16:16

Simon Peter answered, "You are the Christ, the Son of the living God."

SEE JESUS 9

Jesus preaches in his hometown

Luke 4:24

"I tell you the truth," he continued, "no prophet is accepted in his hometown."

SEE JESUS 10

Jesus gathers his disciples

Luke 5:27–28

After this, Jesus went out and saw a tax collector by the name of Levi sitting at his tax booth. "Follow me," Jesus said to him, and Levi got up, left everything and followed him.

SEE JESUS 11

The Sermon on the Mount

Matthew 5:13

"You are the salt of the earth. But if the salt loses its saltiness, how can it be made salty again? It is no longer good for anything, except to be thrown out and trampled by men."

SEE JESUS 12

Jesus sends out his twelve disciples

Matthew 9:37–38

"The harvest is plentiful but the workers are few. Ask the Lord of the harvest, therefore, to send out workers into his harvest field."

SEE JESUS 21

The last supper

Matthew 26:27–28

Then he took the cup, gave thanks and offered it to them, saying, "Drink from it, all of you. This is my blood of the covenant, which is poured out for many for the forgiveness of sins."

SEE JESUS 22

Jesus' trial

John 18:37

"You are a king, then!" said Pilate. Jesus answered, "You are right in saying I am a king. In fact, for this reason I was born, and for this I came into the world, to testify to the truth. Everyone on the side of truth listens to me."

SEE JESUS 23

The crucifixion of Jesus

Luke 23:33–34

When they came to the place called the Skull, there they crucified him, along with the criminals—one on his right, the other on his left.

SEE JESUS 24

The resurrection

John 20:18

Mary Magdalene went to the disciples with the news: "I have seen the Lord!" And she told them that he had said these things to her.

SEE JESUS 17

The transfiguration

Matthew 17:2 (NLT)

As the men watched, Jesus' appearance changed so that his face shone like the sun, and his clothing became dazzling white.

SEE JESUS 18

Jesus is the resurrection and life

John 11:25–26

Jesus said to her, "I am the resurrection and the life. He who believes in me will live, even though he dies; and whoever lives and believes in me will never die."

SEE JESUS 19

Jesus blesses little kids

Matthew 18:3

And he said: "I tell you the truth, unless you change and become like little children, you will never enter the kingdom of heaven."

SEE JESUS 20

The triumphal entry

Matthew 21:9

The crowds that went ahead of him and those that followed shouted, "Hosanna to the Son of David!" "Blessed is he who comes in the name of the Lord!" "Hosanna in the highest!"

SEE JESUS BONUS

God's mercy

Titus 3:4–5

But when the kindness and love of God our Savior appeared, he saved us, not because of righteous things we had done, but because of his mercy.

SEE JESUS 25

Jesus is the way, truth, and life

John 14:6

Jesus answered, "I am the way and the truth and the life. No one comes to the Father except through me."

SEE JESUS BONUS

Jesus fulfills prophecy

Isaiah 53:5

But he was pierced for our transgressions, he was crushed for our iniquities; the punishment that brought us peace was upon him, and by his wounds we are healed.

SEE JESUS BONUS

God's forgiveness

1 John 1:9 (NLT)

But if we confess our sins to him, he is faithful and just to forgive us and to cleanse us from every wrong.

SEE JESUS BONUS

The true identity of Jesus

John 1:1

In the beginning was the Word, and the Word was with God, and the Word was God.

SEE JESUS BONUS

Jesus understands you

Hebrews 4:15

For we do not have a high priest who is unable to sympathize with our weaknesses, but we have one who has been tempted in every way, just as we are—yet was without sin.

SEE JESUS BONUS

The true identity of Jesus

John 1:14 (NLT)

So the Word became human and lived here on earth among us. He was full of unfailing love and faithfulness. And we have seen his glory, the glory of the only Son of the Father.

SEE JESUS BONUS

Believing in Jesus

John 20:31

But these are written that you may believe that Jesus is the Christ, the Son of God, and that by believing you may have life in his name.